Against the Tide

The Billy & Lily O'Neill Story

by IVAN LITTLE

Ivan Little started his journalistic career with the Portadown Times before working in the news and features departments of the Belfast Telegraph. A move into broadcasting took him to Downtown Radio, where he was a news editor and in 1980 he joined Ulster Television where he stayed for 29 years, working extensively too for ITN. Since 2009 he has been an award-winning freelance writer and columnist. He's also an acclaimed actor and Against the Tide is his seventh book.

NSPCC

Proceeds after production costs from the sale of this book

will be donated to NSPCC

and

Ballymoney Rotary Club Local Charities

DESIGN • PRINT • PUBLISHING • DISTRIBUTION

Designed & Published by Cedric Wilson

Email: cedricwilson@live.co.uk

FOREWORD

Billy and Lily O'Neills story beautifully told by award winning broadcaster and journalist Ivan Little can by any standards be regarded as a good read. Their story is a fascinating account of their life experiences over many decades.

It provides a rich tapestry of their family backgrounds. It can also be regarded as a 'love story' which recounts their feelings and ambitions particularly set within the mores that then existed in society in regards to marriage particularly as such was seen as a 'mixed marriage'. It also tells of their times as very accomplished dancers and their ongoing generous support of a range of community based charities particularly through Billy's involvement in the Rotary movement.

I can vouch for the accuracy of the information due to Billy's remarkable encyclopaedic memory and the formidable collection of papers and photographic material maintained over the years. I strongly commend this publication to you and your family and also thank you for purchasing it recognising that several worthy charities will benefit from the funds raised.

Cecil Graham LVO. OBE.

CONTENTS

INTRODUCTION

This is the story of a fighter who wouldn't throw in the towel. The story of Billy O'Neill, a man who consistently beat the odds in his private and business lives. A man who rose from humble beginnings in a small County Antrim town to thrive in the hospitality sector in Northern Ireland where his name has become synonymous with the ever-growing caravan industry particularly around the popular seaside resorts Castlerock and Portstewart which stand about six miles apart on the north coast.

A man from a modest home in the a quirkily named street, the Rodden Foot in Ballymoney who moved up in the world to take on and completely refurbish an impressive mansion that was once compared in the press to TV's Downton Abbey.

A Roman Catholic man who swam against the tide of Northern Ireland's religious taboos and who, ignored familial opposition and eloped to Scotland to marry the love of his life 'from the other side' – Protestantism - Lily Staddon. A man who refused to be bound by sectarian shackles who not only shared his life with Lily, the mother of their two sons, but also relaxed by spending countless hours with her on ballroom floors as the fleet-footed couple skilfully indulged their passion for dancing that would eventually catch the eye of Strictly Come Dancing's Len Goodman and see them waltzing off with awards over the decades.

Yet Billy is something of an accidental millionaire. What he and Lily achieved in their relentless rise through the commercial world wasn't planned with any degree of strategic forethought.

And this book, Against the Tide tells how, after having a number of small-scale jobs in Northern Ireland to earn enough money to help his mother provide for his siblings, Billy moved to England to work in the construction industry before returning to his homeland to pursue similar roles here. And he recalls how his first tentative steps into the tourism industry came with the sub-letting of a single caravan.

But remarkably before long Billy was running two shops and had agency's from major English companies to sell their caravans in Northern Ireland before the enterprising and far sighted businessman started to develop caravan parks.

Billy also reflects on these pages on his joy at building and operating a successful hotel and apartment complex between Portrush and Portstewart though he encountered repeated difficulties with officialdom and his dreams of expansion ultimately ended up in frustration.

The book recounts how all along the way Billy faced torrid battles with the planners as he sought to widen his caravan, hotel and property business. And he also went on the offensive against tourism bosses in Northern Ireland, claiming they were encouraging hospitality firms from outside the province to set up businesses with financial support that wasn't offered to indigenous entrepreneurs.

Billy and Lily still managed to surmount the obstacles in their path to strengthen their remarkable business network that included a string of caravan parks and that aforementioned award winning apartment and hotel complex which became a hub for one of Europe's most successful youth football tournaments – a competition which gave the likes of David Beckham, Paul Scholes and Gary Neville of Manchester United and England their first step on the ladder to soccer stardom.

But there's more to Billy and Lily than their bank balances. They've raised and donated hundreds of thousands of pounds to charities in both communities in Northern Ireland.

And after they scaled back their hectic schedules they used some of their hard earned wealth to travel the globe on cruises and holidays, taking pride in establishing friendships in virtually every corner of the world and spreading the word about the positive side of Northern Ireland, as a must-see destination, far and wide.

Billy has also been acknowledged for his contributions to worldwide humanitarian and charitable organisations like the Rotary Club, the Round Table and the Lions Club, spreading their messages with a fervour and a passion.

All in all, it's been an astonishing journey for Billy and Lily and even though they have rubbed shoulders with royalty - and bizarrely bought furniture that had once been graced by the late eccentric pop megastar Michael Jackson - friends have insisted the O'Neills always had the common touch and could, and did, mix with anyone and everyone. Or as one former resident of the Rodden Foot said: "They were the sort of pair who never lost the run of themselves."

1

Humble beginnings and getting a foothold in the Rodden Foot

A soft County Antrim rain was falling in Ballymoney on that fateful morning in March 1956 when 16 year old Billy O'Neill took his first uncertain steps into the unknown. Wearing a blue trench-coat, buttoned up tight against the unpredictable weather, Billy had only a small brown suitcase with him as Jeannie O'Neill, the mother he worshipped, saw him across the road to his hometown's 101 year old railway station to begin his voyage of discovery to England. And the words of wisdom she whispered tearfully to him never left him. Jeannie was a happy-go-lucky woman who was always ready with a song or a quip but Billy noticed a different side

Leo O'Neill age 16

to his mother that day. Wrapping her arms around him, Jeannie apologised that she and her late husband Ned hadn't been able to give Billy the education they thought he deserved but she added: "You don't have to go to university to learn that good manners and honesty will take you just as far as a degree." And with that her youngest son was gone - on a journey that would take him the length and breadth of Britain as he helped in the construction of motorways and back home to Northern Ireland where Billy would one day soar to the top of the hospitality industry, a success story that would eventually earn him what friends celebrated as a richly deserved MBE from the Queen, not just for his business acumen but also for his charitable and community work for every imaginable good cause in Northern Ireland and beyond.

But not even Billy could have imagined what lay ahead as he said his farewells to Jeannie in Ballymoney –known by locals as The Toon - where, bizarrely, a monkey called Mickey; a pony named Donald and a young ice cream lover called Ian Paisley had all played pivotal roles in his formative years up to that date.

Not to mention a world war, the religious divisions which bedevilled his native Northern Ireland and a teacher who dismissively told Billy he would never amount to anything in life.

Which could scarcely have been further from the truth for this self-made man who'd come into the world when the Second World War, which was to ravage Europe, was only 85 days old. He was one of eight boys and three girls who were the products of a mixed marriage between a Protestant and a Roman Catholic, the same sort of marital union that was to cause strife in his own life many years later.

A birth certificate recorded that William Weir O'Neill was born on Monday, November 27, 1939. His father was Edward 'Ned' O'Neill, a Roman Catholic from Ballymena and Jeannie Ramsey, a Protestant from Armoy, a tiny village that was to gain worldwide fame many years later as the home of the all-conquering motorcycle racing dynasty, the Dunlops..

And not far away from Armoy today, thousands of visitors are drawn to the area from all over the world to see and photograph the Dark Hedges, an avenue of intertwining beech trees made famous in the epic TV series Game of Thrones which was filmed largely in Northern Ireland.

Like Billy his own father had come from a big family. Billy's grandfather David had married three times. But Billy doesn't remember him or his grandmother Elizabeth that everyone knew as Lizzie.

Billy's parents had met in the bustling town of Ballymena and they were married in the Church of Our Lady & St John in the heart of the tiny village of Dervock, not far from Ballymoney.

Weddings across the religious divide in Northern Ireland were often frowned upon in those days and completely divided families but Billy remembers his Protestant grandad Hugh Ramsey visiting the family home at the Rodden Foot in Ballymoney on the morning of a Twelfth of July celebration of the anniversary of King William of Orange winning the Battle of the Boyne in County Meath in 1690.

His grandad was wearing a massive Orange sash and he gave his grandchildren a half a crown each and told his daughter Jeannie, who had a twin brother and three sisters that even though she had changed her religion to Catholicism she was still his favourite.

Hugh owned a popular grocery shop in Castle Street in Ballymoney which is now the site of a memorial garden to members of the aforementioned racing Dunlops who died in tragic accidents during races.

Billy remembers that people could have bought anything and everything from his grandfather who moved his business to Armoy where fruit, hardware, and even antiques were always on sale.

He also recalls that Hugh kept a monkey called Mickey in the shop to attract customers inside.

Hugh also had a small horse, a jennet called Donald, and a spring cart that he used to meet his transport needs.

Billy says: "Grandad's favourite days of the year were the days of the 'Oul Lammas Fair in Ballycastle which drew tens of thousands of people to the town every August. He would take Donald there and offer £10 to anyone who could stay on its back for two minutes. If they couldn't they had to give granddad £5 so not surprisingly he always ended with a lot of fivers!

"When Granddad Hugh died on October 22, 1952 he bequeathed Donald to my mother. Johnny Mulholland, my stepfather, could not control it so my mother gave it to young Albert McKay the blacksmith. He was the only person who could handle Donald and Albert kept it in a stable behind Phil Donoghue's pub in Market Street."

Granny Lizzie who died in 1937 is buried in Roseyards churchyard with her son James. Granddad Hugh who died in 1952 had requested to be buried in Armoy Presbyterian church graveyard, where many years later Billy arranged for a headstone to be erected.

Billy was the youngest of the O'Neill boys, Leo, Hughie, Eddie, David, Jack, and two sons called James, one of whom died as an infant. Billy's three sisters were called Ruby, Jean, and Elizabeth who all married servicemen.

Life for the O'Neills was difficult during the war years especially after the sudden death of the head of the family Ned in England, leaving his widow to bring up a large family on little income which was supplemented by what Billy's brothers could send home from jobs across the water.

Billy's earliest memory of the war is of American soldiers in the recreation hall of Trinity church just across the road from his home. He says: "It was full of GIs and I remember them throwing bubble gum, sweets and threepence pieces to the kids in the street. They scrambled for them and I later heard that some of the soldiers also handed the odd packet of nylons to the older girls in Ballymoney.

Billy's Mother Jeannie O'Neill   Billy's Father Edward O'Neill

Twin half sisters Sheila/Marie and Anne Teresa Mulholland

Billy O'Neill, Mary Mulholland, Elizabeth O'Neill, James O'Neill

4

"I also remember there were families from Belfast who came to live in Ballymoney and there were quite a number of children who had been evacuated from the bombings in the city."

Billy started school on his fourth birthday and his older siblings James and Jack took him there on his first day.

Also starting at St Patrick's school that day was a teacher called Master John McKeown who was never among Billy's favourite tutors even though he acknowledged that he was extremely good at his job.

"He was really strict especially about time-keeping," says Billy. "I was never that punctual. nor that clever. I didn't like reading or spelling though I was okay at arithmetic and history but I couldn't envisage earning money in later life telling stories about history.

"At one point I stayed away from school because Master McKeown was giving off to me so much for being late. The reason for my poor timekeeping was that I was always helping with the family ice-cream making business. A few days later my oldest brother Leo brought me back to school again. I used to take a short cut to school along Edward Street and Henry Street but when I was about 10 years old a boy who was a lot bigger than me always tried to stop me. One snowy day I decided that I'd had enough and that I wasn't going to allow him to bully me anymore. I started to fight him and when we were both on the ground his older sister came out and gave him a couple of slaps on his ear and told him to let me go to school. He never bothered me again."

Billy who had started school on his birthday left ten years later on his 14th birthday. And the admonishment of Master McKeown still rings in his ears. For the teacher told him: "You will do nothing and you will go nowhere"

Billy asked the master why he'd said that. "And he replied: 'Okay, let me ask you this - If you had £2-10s in your left trouser pocket and £2-10s in your right trouser pocket what would you have?' I joked that I would have someone else's trousers on."

Billy was, however in a roundabout way, to have Master McKeown to thank for introducing him to a pastime that would bring him happiness that would last for the rest of his life.

The teacher used to run dances in Ballymoney Town Hall to raise money for a new school, Our Lady of Lourdes and he hired the best showbands in Ireland to play at them.

Billy went along as much out of curiosity as anything else but he quickly found out that he loved to dance, with the jive and jitter-bug his favourites. One of his earliest partners was a girl called Lily but not the Lily he would one day marry. The 'first' Lily was called Lily Peacock – a cousin of Glasgow Celtic and Northern Ireland footballing legend Bertie Peacock – but the young dancers soon landed in hot water.

The two youngsters were dancing energetically in the Town Hall and Billy threw Lily over his head, turning other heads in the process because she was wearing a short black skirt with a split which revealed quite a bit of flesh.

The other dancers applauded him but Master McKeown stopped Billy and Lily in their tracks, warning them that a priest, Father McGorrian who was due to arrive in the Town Hall would not be amused and the teacher ordered them to desist from any more of what he called 'that devil dancing.'

Many years later Master McKeown and Billy would meet again in Coleraine – at a Holmes Cash and Carry store. By that time Billy was the proud owner of three caravan parks, three shops and O'Neill's Causeway Coast Hotel and holiday apartment complex in Portrush with a workforce of more than 100 people.

In the Cash-and-Carry Master McKeown approached Billy and the pair shook hands with the former teacher congratulating his ex-pupil on the success he had made of his life and eating his words that he would amount to nothing.

Twenty-eight years after Master McKeown had held the prestigious role of President of Ballymoney Rotary Club, Billy too was to become the proud wearer of the chain of office.

Billy says that while he may not always have seen eye to eye with Master McKeown he will never forget the role he played in his life. By coincidence his former teacher is buried in the same church graveyard that is his mother Jeannie's final resting place.

"When I visit my mother's grave I stop and say a few words for Master McKeown and his wife Rose Teresa," says Billy who smiles as he recalls how his teacher as well as his priests used to wonder how he got his Christian name at a time when many young kids brought up in the catholic faith were named after saints.

"They knew there wasn't a Saint William or Billy and that King William of Orange was the only William that they ever heard of, but they didn't think I was called after him! But I said I was very happy to be called after my father's best friend William Weir. I still laugh about what they would have made of me marrying Orange Lily in later life!"

Billy's first home had been at 42 Meetinghouse Street Ballymoney but his family moved to 16 Rodden Foot, a two up, two down dwelling which was one of a row of 22 cottage type houses in the street.

A history book on Ballymoney includes a photograph of the Rodden Foot and explains that it was taken prior to the demolition of the houses in 1958. The narrative says "It started out as a 'clachan' of houses at the foot of a rodden – a river – outside the town. By the time it was opened the Rodden Foot had become an important entry street in Ballymoney due to the 'new road' which had been cut from Ballymena to Coleraine, passing through the centre of the old clachan site. Although not far from the town of Ballymoney the Rodden Foot was very much a separate unit with its own shops and its own way of life. "

Billy concurs with the words accompanying the picture, saying: "The Rodden Foot was like a village within a town." And he can rhyme off the names of the characters who lived there including the O'Neills' neighbours like the shop-owning ancestors of Keith and Kristyn Getty, the Ulster-born couple who are massively successful stars on the American gospel music scene but who also maintain their local roots by coming home to Northern Ireland during the summer months to a house they own on the north coast.

The Rodden Foot

Grandfather Hugh Ramsey

David O'Neill, Desmond Mulholland

Among Billy's treasured keepsakes of the Rodden Foot are a series of photographs of the former residents of the street including one of a party of families celebrating the Festival of Britain in 1951. But also in the collection is a picture of Billy's mother Jeannie with twin daughters Sheila Marie and Ann Teresa she bore at the age of 49 to her second husband, Johnny Mulholland.

Two other photographs are important ones for Billy, including ones that recall the O'Neill's family business, making their own fondly remembered brand of ice cream. One picture shows Billy's brother Leo selling ice cream from a specially adapted three-wheeled cart and another one of the ice cream factory that Jeannie and son Hughie built.

A painting of the O'Neills' Rodden Foot dwelling by popular Ballymoney-born artist and former Portora Royal School, Enniskillen teacher Hugh McIlfatrick and which was given to Billy on his 60th birthday hangs proudly in his home overlooking Portstewart golf club and the magnificent strand beyond.

All around the house too there are pictures, old and new, which illustrate just how important Billy and Lily's family are to them. And there are also certificates and posters which underline the contributions that the O'Neills have made to the tourism industry in Northern Ireland and to their local communities in Ballymoney, Coleraine, Portrush, Portstewart and Castlerock.

There are also evocative reminders of the O'Neills' ice cream business and how it went from strength to strength and how their Rodden Foot home was extended by Billy's father to include an ice house so that he could improve his trade, using a recipe that was apparently left to him by an Italian in Ballymena whom he had befriended.

One man who was employed as a youngster in the ice cream operation was the late William P.O'Kane JP OBE who later went on to establish the hugely renowned O'Kane's poultry processing company, one of the largest businesses of its kind.

Billy O'Neill's father wasn't afraid of hard work and he started his job at 4am seven days a week, selling his ice cream from St Patrick's Day in March until Halloween in October.

In the cold winter months people, not surprisingly, shunned ice creams and the O'Neills had to eke out their summer earnings to cover their outgoings for the whole year.

The ice cream was prepared by Jeannie, who Billy remembers always wore a pristine white apron, using a complicated process which involved steel cylinders and wooden barrels packed with dry ice topped with a special salt designed to stop it melting.

"Each batch contained eight gallons of ice-cream, which sold for £8 and was offered to the public in sliders, cones or pokes for between one and three old pennies" says Billy. "I was the 'go for' brother who had to – as the name suggests - go for the ingredients for the ice-cream and had to do messages for my older siblings. If the weather was bad and the ice cream didn't sell it was destroyed and fresh batches were made the next day."

The people of North Antrim quickly 'warmed' to the O'Neills' ice cream. Billy's father had started selling it from a hand cart around Ballymoney but as its popularity grew he upgraded to a pony and cart to take his wares to the neighbouring towns of Portrush, Portstewart, Kilrea, Garvagh, Bushmills, Portballintrae, Ballycastle and even across the mountain to the villages of Cushendun and Cushendall.

Soon however one pony and cart wasn't enough to meet the demands and before long there was a fleet of them – all brightly painted - on the road.

Billy's oldest brother Leo also sold ice cream from a specially adapted three-wheeled cycle which he would ride up to 25 miles every day.

And the strenuous work was said to have given Leo the perfect training for the fight of his life on one occasion when against the odds, he lifted the Ulster light heavyweight boxing championship, an achievement celebrated around Ballymoney by the lighting of bonfires.

One battle the O'Neills couldn't win, however, was the one to save their ice-cream business from closure. The outbreak of war in 1939 and the subsequent difficulties in acquiring ingredients delivered knock-out blows.

But Ned O'Neill fought back. Along with a number of other men from around the area known as the Route, he volunteered to go to Barrow-in -Furness in England to rebuild roofs on factories bombed by the Germans.

However tragically at the age of just 46 he died of pleurisy on February 27, 1941. Leo who was 17 and was working in Barnard Castle (made infamous in later years by Boris Johnson's former right hand man Dominic Cummings) was the only member of the O'Neill family who could attend the funeral.

Billy says: "The people of the Rodden Foot were a great comfort to my mother who was left with ten children, the youngest Elizabeth who was just 16 days old. I was only 15 months old."

Billy remembers his mother, who was diabetic and had to inject herself with insulin twice a day, as an extremely generous woman who would go out of her way to help people and who sometimes cooked Ulster fries for strangers who knocked on her door.

Jeannie O'Neill was also a resourceful and determined woman and after the war ended and ingredients became more available she and Billy's brothers decided the time was right to re-start the ice cream manufacturing.

She was married again to a man called Johnny Mulholland who was tasked with looking after the horses and carts for their ice-cream selling travels and travails.

Leo came back from England and he, Hughie, David, Jack and James all had horses and carts while Billy, who was 14, would give his brothers a hand on Saturdays and Sundays.

"But I had to have a driver as I was too young to be in charge of a horse. My mother hired one of our neighbours John Tweed and my journey took in a number of places around the town, ending up on the Dunloy Road where there were a number of housing estates," says Billy whose brother Eddie helped his mum to make the ice cream.

One of the O'Neills' prized acquisitions was a beautiful Italian ice cream cart from an Italian man called Johnny Marcella in Portrush.

Hughie and his wife Joan

Elizabeth and Bob McKee

St Patrick's Girls School

James and Rita

Jack and Rosemary

David and Florence

Hughie and Joan

11

A picture of the ornate cart which Hughie bought because he was so enthralled with its carved roses, diamond-shaped mirrors and four poles holding up the canopy, is another of Billy's treasured possessions in his Portstewart home. Sadly the cart was destroyed when its frisky horse, called Dick, bolted outside a shop and hit a telegraph pole after it was spooked by the sound of a farmer starting up his tractor.

Happily there were funnier times too. Billy says a boy once asked Hughie in the village of Clough outside Ballymoney for a free ice cream and in return the youngster bizarrely said he would curse the Pope loudly and often. But happily the boy also spread the word about how good the pokes and sliders were – and sales of the O'Neills' ice-cream doubled.

Many years later Billy told the story to DUP politician Ian Paisley junior who passed it on to his father the late First Minister at Stormont, the Rev Ian RK Paisley who was said to have laughed heartily. The veteran politician and Free Presbyterian Church Moderator, who was known to have had something of a sweet tooth, also revealed that he had been a huge fan in his younger days of O'Neills' ice cream, rating it as the best in Ireland.

The ever-resourceful Hughie turned a 1936 Ford 8 car into an ice cream van but with business booming in 1950 Jeannie decided to build a factory in Edward Street not far from the Rodden Foot.

However the new venture was doomed. Major national ice cream makers Walls and Lyons were putting free fridges into shops in towns and villages to sell their products and the O'Neills had decided to close their business down.

Leo, Hughie and Eddie went to work in Scotland on the Hydro Electric Tunnel scheme with other workmen from the Ballymoney area.

Hughie later moved to Rochester in Kent where he worked for Sir Robert McAlpine on the construction of the BP oil refinery on the Isle of Grain before becoming a stevedore on the River Medway and he met and married an American woman called Joan Gouder who presented him with three children.

Billy recalls that while Hughie may have departed from Ballymoney his love of ice-cream stayed with him. He had his own ice cream machine in his home and he famously recounted the story to Billy of how he once ate 22 ice creams in one day.

Billy says Hughie looked like the former Goon Show comedian, singer and all-round entertainer Harry Secombe and like him had a good singing voice. Such was his reputation and his repertoire of Irish songs that he was often invited onstage as a guest by the likes of the Dubliners, the Wolfe Tones and the Clancy Brothers.

Eddie had been the first of the boys to be married. His bride was Mary McLarnon from Armoy and Billy remembers his mother singing her favourite songs at the reception in Tillie Malloy's upstairs barn. Jack joined the Army and with his wife Rosemary settled in Hertfordshire.

Billy says that he has only happy memories of growing up in the Rodden Foot. "It was a nice safe place to live. Our front door was never locked," he adds. And an affectionate poem about the Rodden Foot was written after the old houses on the street were demolished. (A copy of the poem is included towards the end of this book)

Billy's best friends were Jim Wilson, Billy Wade, Francis Mills and Jimmy Taggart who regularly went to the local cinema together to see cowboy films with stars of the day like Hopalong Cassidy, Roy Rodgers, Gene Autry and the Durango Kid.

It wasn't unusual says Billy for an old man called Francis McGuinness in the heart of the auditorium to shout out warnings to the onscreen 'good guys ' if a 'baddie' was about to shoot them. The manager of the cinema Bob Kane, whose nickname was The Rancher, often threatened to throw Francis out on his ear but Billy says he thought twice because patrons frequently enjoyed the interjections more than the movies.

Billy and his pals used to play football – with a pig's bladder for a ball – and cricket and rounders on a nettle and thistles filled green behind the Rodden Foot houses where the space would also see horses grazing along with chickens and pigs.

Sara Adams bred cattle nearby in Edward Street and businesses in the area included a funeral parlour and a blacksmith's as well as a bicycle repair shop and a not-very-well-stocked grocery shop owned by an elderly man called Beau Jamison who had an eye for Billy's sister to whom he would regularly send a bar of Cadbury's Milk Tray via her brother as a token of his affection.

It's a memory which after many years still gives Jean (who will be 90yrs of age in June 2022) a laugh.

The Rodden Foot green was also home to a regular gathering of poker players and a pitch and toss school, both of which were regularly raided by the Royal Ulster Constabulary before the seven or eight card sharps finally found another base in the home of a woman called Annie Barr who lived on her own.

Billy used to run errands for the poker players and one night he was invited to join them at the table because there was a shortage of participants for the game.

 Billy recalls: "I said 'yes' not telling them I had only two shillings on me but I won the first hand. And my luck was really in that night because I won over £13 and after school the next day I went up to Robert Gamble's drapery shop in Church St and bought my first suit with long trousers for £10 though my mother gave off to me after she had found out I had been playing cards. I kept the other £3 to join the card school the next Sunday but they wouldn't let me take part, though they still let me do the messages."

Billy's stepfather Johnny who kept greyhounds enjoyed a flutter, much to his wife's displeasure and his stepson once found £200 of his winnings in the dry toilet behind their home. His reward? Half a crown.

Johnny and Billy's mother had four children of their own, Mary, Desmond and twins Sheila Marie and Anne Teresa. "There were so many of us it's safe to say the dry toilet never got cold," laughs Billy.

Brother Hughie

Brother Leo

Billy's Father Edward O'Neill

O'Neill ice-cream factory

Mother Jeannie and stepfather Johnny Mulholland

Billy aged 12

Eddie and Mary O'Neill- First of the family to Marry in Armoy circa 1950

2

Turkeys, pigs, a henduck and dancing to a new beat

A s one door closes, another one opens, they say. And so it was with Billy O'Neill. When his family's ice- cream business shut down the 14-year-old youngster was determined to keep himself busy. So he started to deliver the Belfast Telegraph newspaper for Morrison's news-agency beside the Palladium cinema and his round, on foot, covered a large part of Ballymoney six early evenings a week for which he was paid the princely sum of five shillings.

For four years before the paper round Billy had worked for Frank Skelton's timber box manufacturing firm in Edward Street. The boxes were used to export chickens, turkeys and geese to England by the Duffin and Flemings poultry business.

Palladium Cinema Ballymoney

Star Ballroom, Maidstone, Kent, 1957

First visit to Margate

Teddy Boy suit

Brother Eddie and Mathew Coyles

Brother Leo 1955

Jack O'Neill on service, Cyprus

Leo, Ulster Light Heavyweight 1946

Jack O'Neill serving at Aldershot

Says Billy who was only a child at the time says: "My job was to carry the timber slats to the men making the boxes. I also brushed the floors and lifted any spare nails around the place. I did that for one hour a day after school and two hours on a Saturday morning when we all got paid. For me it was 2s 6d but I also got chocolates from brothers Jimmy and Tommy McClelland for doing messages for them.

Billy took over another job from his brother Jack who used to walk greyhounds for Sammy Duffin for whom he later plucked turkeys, chicken and geese in the run-up to Christmas.

Billy says that Sammy's brother Clark was a great story teller who once claimed he had bred a chicken with a duck and the resultant 'henduck' had a web-foot and a claw-foot which made it swim in circles as it crowed cock-a- doodle-do-quack-quack!

Billy's next job was at Stevensons' pork factory in Ballymoney. His role was to scrape the hair off butchered pigs' legs and prepare the hams for smoking in a special room with a fire pit in the middle and a window to let the smoke out. By that stage he was earning £1.10s but Billy wasn't happy there and his mother suggested that he should apply for a job in Balnamore flax spinning mill where she had worked as a 12-year-old and where as an under-age employee she used to have to hide in large containers when health inspectors came calling.

Billy got a job in the Balnamore number two spinning room, working five days a week from 8am to 6pm for £3 and with free transport to and from the Rodden Foot he was 'over the moon.'

The record books show that in the early 19th Century, Balnamore was one of the largest spinning mills outside Belfast. In its prime, it employed more than 400 people. Despite the harsh conditions, local people who were employed there remember it as a good place to work, a place with a strong sense of community.

Billy was fascinated with the mill's history and his research showed that its roots went back to 1764 when a man called John Caldwell bought a corn mill and 40 acres of land at a place known as Harmony Hill, later to be named Balnamore. Caldwell added a bleach works and small beetling mill and was soon running a profitable business. The mill later came under the control of Joseph Bryan. He installed 400 water-powered spindles and began making strong yarn for sail cloth and canvas. A village began to grow up around the mill, with houses for employees, a shop and a school. In later years, there was even a football team. The mill was sold to Braidwater Spinning Company Ltd., of Ballymena, who extended it and introduced new water-powered turbines. In the 1920s, it was sold again, to Hale, Martin & Co. Ltd

"I enjoyed working in the mill," Billy says. "I gave my mother £2 from my wages for my keep and spent the other pound on sweets or ice cream. I was assigned in the number two spinning mill to assist a spinner called Effie Hartin who was my next door neighbour in the Rodden Foot. I was called a cage boy and I had to collect the full bobbins which the spinners placed on 12 bobbin spikes. The cages were then taken to what was known as the 'reeling room'."

Most of the employees at the time were female and Billy recalls that young boys like him were the targets for repeated good-natured pranks. But on a serious note he remembers that the employees had to work in their bare feet because the hot water from wet spinning frames would destroy their footwear.

The only daily breaks in the mill were 45 minutes for lunch and two 10 minute tea breaks. Billy was promoted – for no extra money - to 'flyer boy' at the mill which involved soldering work in a separate room and he admits he was lonely there, away from the hustle and bustle of his former workplace.

A year later more promotion came – again with no increase in pay – when Billy was moved to the fluting room where at least he was able to help Ross Fleming who became his best friend.

The fluting was a repairing process performed on the mill's mill rolls when they were worn out and it could be an arduous task. But Billy recalls that he and Ross one day went fishing for eels in a nearby stream and were two minutes late back to their posts, costing them a half day's pay for their tardiness which was never repeated.

There were laughs a plenty in the mill and Billy joined the Army cadets with some of his mill colleagues including Danny McKay, Billy Wade, Reggie Tweed, Jim and John Riley, Joe Bo McVicker, John Laverty, and Johnny McDowell some of whom went on a trip together to Altcar in England.

The friends also enjoyed cycling outings nearer home with Billy on a Vaux Popular racer that cost him five shillings a month. The destinations included Kilrea, Coleraine, Portstewart and Portrush for fireworks displays. But after one excursion Billy was shocked to find that his prized bike which he'd lent to Joe Bo McVicker to get him home was covered with blood.

Billy imagined all sorts of dreadful things but Joe Bo explained the gore by saying he had seen a dead hare by the side of the road and slung it over the handlebars of the bike to cook it for his greyhounds.

It was during his time in the Army cadets that Billy got a deeper appreciation, and love, of dancing.

He and a group of colleagues were returning from a day's shooting practice at Ballykinlar army base in County Down and decided to go to the cinema to watch the John Wayne/Maureen O'Hara film The Quiet Man which was set in Ireland.

But the queue for the cinema was too long and the young men couldn't get in, prompting one of their number to suggest that they should go instead to the local Orange Hall where there was a dance on.

Says Billy: "Johnny McBride's band were playing and it was the first time I had been to an actual dance. I was enjoying the music and fun when two girls Mary McToal and Kathleen Wallace who worked in the mill, tried to encourage me onto the dance floor. I was reluctant because I was wearing big boots but the girls wouldn't take no for an answer and the ice was broken.

School photo with Master McKeown and Miss Mullan

St Patrick's football team Leo O'Neill goalkeeper with Master McQuillan

Balnamore Flax Spinning Mill

The Quiet Man Movie

"I stayed up for the Canadian Barn Dance plus an old time waltz and a quick step."

And that was Billy hooked on dancing which would become a life-time love. Before long he was going to dances in Orange Halls in Cloughmills and Drumaheglis, before he progressed to the Boat House in Coleraine, the Palais de Dance in Portstewart as well as Town Halls including the civic centres in Ballymena and Ballymoney.

Dancing became Billy's main hobby and he was literally following in the footsteps of his older brothers and sisters who were all good dancers.

He remembers one night when he was nearly 16 he went to a dance in Coleraine Town Hall wearing the 'cool' garb of the time - his first drain pipe trousers, black shirt, slim Jim tie and green corduroy jacket.

The outfit caught the eye of a 'lovely girl who looked like a Barbie doll' called Nancy Davies. She asked Billy up for a quick step, saying she had danced before with his brother Hughie who also enjoyed the company on the dance floor with dwarfs who were employed by Barry's amusements to man a miniature village where a ghost train was later installed.

Billy's fascination with dancing was anything but small-time. And at dances on the North Coast he had a regular group of partners including Cissie Marrs, Edith Logan, Lily Peacock and Maura Hays, who married his good friend Maurice Penny. For Billy there was no romance with any of his regular dance partners because they were all older than him.

3

Trouble at Mill and a new life in England

Life was looking good for Billy at the mill until one day in March 1956 when he was among 16 workers who were paid off in what was the beginning of the end for the mill as well. Billy knew that desperate times needed desperate measures. And he decided to go to live with his brother Hughie and his wife Joan in England where he hoped to find work. Billy sold a watch that his brother David had given him for £4.10s to his stepfather to pay for the journey on the Heysham boat and bade farewell to his mother who hugged and kissed him before expressing regret that she and his father hadn't been able to give him the education they wanted for him.

Working on the M1 between Rugby and Leicester

But she gave Billy that priceless advice on the doorstep. "She told me to remember two things that would take me far – good manners and honesty which she said didn't require a university education. It was advice that I never forgot from my mother who was a hard working woman, who reared 14 children and was always humming and singing and coming out with funny sayings. But she was a woman of action too. "One day when I was only eight years old she caught me smoking a butt of a cigarette and promptly marched me to Kenneth Getty's shop and bought a packet of five Woodbines. She told me to have a good smoke and I got through two and a half of them before I felt so awful that I resolved I would never smoke again. And I never did."

Billy's brother Jack accompanied him to Hughie's home in Rochester in Kent where Leo lived too before leaving his job as a concrete foreman on a new bridge over the River Medway to go to work in Scotland.

Another brother was also there and brother-in-law Jimmy Donnelly who was married to Billy's sister Jean also showed up. He was a captain in the Merchant Navy and his tanker was unloading in Tilbury docks.

Jimmy had once asked Billy if he would be interested in a job on his ship as a junior engineer. The reply was a firm 'no' because Billy knew he was prone to sea sickness.

Tragedy lay ahead for Jimmy. On March 4, 1983 the night of the 21st birthday of Billy's son Terry in the Londonderry Hotel, Portrush, Jimmy, a father of seven children, complained that he was unwell.

After several days in hospitals in Ballymoney and Belfast Jimmy died as Billy was driving his sister Jean to visit him along with her daughter Katherine and her husband Al.

But long before that in England, Billy took Hughie's advice to seek a job with McAlpine's on a £54m contract at the BP oil refinery at the Isle of Grain where he was working.

Alongside Billy was Hughie's father-in-law Charlie Gouder who was the last living survivor of the Lusitania disaster in 1915 when the ocean liner was torpedoed by the German Navy off Kinsale in the Republic of Ireland with the loss of 1197 lives.

What saved Charlie, ironically, was ice cream. He'd gone up on deck to eat one and saw the incoming torpedo and also witnessed the second explosion of the ammunition. Charlie, who was Maltese, had also worked on board the Lusitania's sister ship Mauritania as a cabin steward.

Billy who'd wanted to be a mechanic/fitter working on earth moving machinery and tipper lorries actually got a job as a store man on the McAlpine's project, signing out tools to workers. It was, he says, a tough job, requiring Billy to work a seven day week, receiving £16 in his pay after deductions. It was a lot more than what he'd earned in the mill and he gave Hughie and Joan £4 a week for his keep and sent £3 back home to his mother.

He says: "I loved working on the Isle of Grain. I was one of 5,000 people on the construction and most of them came from southern Ireland, especially Dublin, Connemara and Donegal. It was the first time I heard the Irish language spoken so fluently. And in small world fashion some of the men knew my brothers and my father. After the crude oil tankers off-loaded their cargos at the refinery, mosquitoes could be seen flying up from the tanks and it was said it was the only place in the UK where you could catch malaria.

"The canteens, one for BP workers, the other for contractors were massive, catering for 2,000 employees at a time and on wet days they became like casinos for card games and other forms of gambling."

Fleets of buses brought the workers to the Isle of Grain but there was also a camp on site, full of wooden huts which were home to mainly Irish workers and some were notorious for being rowdy.

Billy didn't enjoy the isolation of the store job but from the half door of the facility he was able to watch – a little enviously – as fitters did their repairs and on one occasion the boss Jim Travers asked him to wash his car, a 1948 Vauxhall, telling him he was going in it to meet the Queen. Billy also volunteered for the spare-time task of repairing ex-Army and Royal Air Force bicycles that a team of 40 time-keepers used to transport them around the four mile square site.

Billy was nicknamed 'The Bicycle Mechanical Engineer' and his boss Mr. Travers was so impressed by his efforts that he offered to enrol him on a mechanical apprenticeship at a nearby technical college one day a week. But as that would have meant him losing £8 from his pay packet, Billy turned down the chance to go to the tech on a Friday because the financial cut would have hit the money he could send home to his mother.

Instead Billy accepted a job as a fitter's mate which didn't impact on his wages and offered not only promotion and an increase in pay but also a certification after five years, as well as requiring him to join the Transport and General Workers Union.

Says Billy: "I worked with a man called Vincent Adams to March 1960, starting first of all on the Bedford tipping lorries reconditioning engines before moving to, among other things, international diggers JCB and Ruston Bucyrus, the world's biggest excavator manufacturer."

One lorry driver who brought his vehicle for repairs to the firm's massive workshop, which was like an aircraft hangar, was a fascinating man from Belfast called Sean Russell for whom Billy acted as a 'conductor' ringing the bell to stop and start a bus bringing workers for free to and from their work.

Sean had been a rear gunner on a bomber in the RAF during World War Two and he promised to take Billy up on a plane during the next commemorations of the Battle of Britain. But sadly the flight never got off the ground because Sean died after his bus collided with a hay lorry in Chatham.

"I was totally devastated, I went home thinking of his wife and three small children who I never met until his funeral in Rainham Cemetery where my brother James would later be buried too," says Billy whose first holiday back home came at Easter 1957 when he re-kindled his love affair with dancing, firstly at an Orange Hall in Portrush which was the venue for a popular jive session. Playing the music there was a jazz band led by Billy White who was later to become musical director with Ulster Television in Belfast.

Ronny Scott's Jazz Club

Louis Armstrong and Jimmy Compton

Louis Armstrong and Ella Fitzgerald

Kenny Ball and his Jazzmen

Dancehall Sweethearts

Dancehalls

Ballymoney Orange Hall]
Ballymoney Town Hall
Ballymena Town Hall
Coleraine Town Hall
Newry Town Hall
Dundalk Town Hall
Armagh City Hall
W.point Town Hall
Ireland Chatham Town Hall
L.Derry Guild Hall
Cork Jazz Festival
L.Derry Jazz //

Boathouse Coleraine
Cloonavin Coleraine
Palais De Dance P.S.
Top Hat Ballroom P.S.
Strand // P.S.
Arcadia Ballroom P.R.
Palladium // P.R.
Flamingo // B.M.
Muff // D.G.
Pageant // Kent
Casino // //
Co Op Rochester //
Co Op Gravesend //
Co Op Chatham //
Ronnie Scotts London
Hammersmith Palais //
Lyceum Ballroom //
Royal Albert Hall //
Cotton Club Glasgow
Locarno B.R. //
Roseland B.R.New York
Cruise New Orleans Jazz Clubs
Las Vegas Hotels
Cruise Ships
CRaic on the Cruise 48
Anna
23 Sept 2008

Bands

Hugh Tourish
Clipper Carlton
Johnnie Quigley
Royal Show Band
Dave Glover Band
Capital S.Band
Cadets //
Chris Barbour Jazz Bd
Acker Bilk
Kemiy Ball
Cy Laurie
Ken Coylier
Alex Welsh
Graham Stewart // //
Paddy Cole // //
Eric Delany Big Band
Joe Loss // //
Ted Heath // //
John Anderson // //
Clyde Valley Stumpers

Jimmy Compton A.S.
Wood Choppers S B.
Monty Sunshine
Original Dixieland J B.
Lonnie Donnagan
And Many Others
Apex Jazz Band
Billy White Jazz Band
George Melly
Stephin Capellie

We danced to Music Of
Glen Miller
Louis Armstrong
Ct Bessie
Jelly Roll Morton
Duke Ellington
Barrel House Jazz Band ??
Jive Five

Favourite Dance No's

In the Mood
The Saints G M In
Sth Rampart St Par
Tiger Rag
Skin Deep
Ice Cream
Marching Th Georgi
Royal Gd Blues
Woodchoppers Ball
High Society
Whistling Rufus
Dident He Ramble
Jazz Ball
Jitterbug Boogie
Chimes Blues
Equinox J M Gar
Hiawatha Rag
Little Brown Jug
Wonderful World
Don't Fence Me In
Guitar Boogie Shu
Jump at Jive

Cherry Pink
Lady in Red
Dancing Queen
Dance the Night Ay
Twist
Cha Cha
Skiffle
Latin American
Be Bop
GI Boogie.
Bugle Boy Boogie

Nights and Days to remember Met Lily 19th May 1960
Easter 1958 Portrush Billy White on lorry around Town to
Orange Hall Jam at Give
Session 3 to 5pm
Palladium Ballroom Portrush Crazy Night Jimmy Compton
All Stars Horse E.T.C.

The Palladium ballroom in Causeway Street in Portrush was another hot spot for dancing especially on what was billed as 'Crazy Night' and certainly lived up to its name whenever Jimmy Compton's All Stars jazz band were on stage.

The first time Billy saw Jimmy he was – believe it or not - playing his trumpet while riding a horse and wearing goggles and flippers. The poor horse however got into trouble and its legs were splayed out to the sides before the other musicians helped it back up again and led it away.

Not long afterwards Jimmy Compton and his band accompanied the legendary jazz musician Louis Armstrong on his tour around Ireland but sadly for Billy he was back working in England and didn't see him though someone got him a photograph of Jimmy with Satchmo whose statue he would later visit in New Orleans

Back in the day in England jazz became a big part of Billy's life. He says: "Over the following three years a group of us would visit all the jazz clubs and dance halls in the Medway towns to hear Chris Barbour, Acker Bilk, Kenny Ball, The Clyde Valley Stompers, The Graham Stewart Seven, Ken Collier, The Monty Sunshine Band, George Melly and Dizzy Gillespie."

Billy danced regularly with partners like Barbra Cummings, Jean Connelly and Christine Bannfield who were part of the crowd who even went to the Royal Albert Hall in London for an all-night jazz band ball with the musicians they all knew so well.

They also went to the acclaimed Ronnie Scott's jazz club in the centre of London but the more modern brand of music wasn't great for dancing, according to Billy though in another venue, the 11 Steps he was able to hear the pioneers of skiffle music like Lonnie Donegan and Nancy Whiskey.

Billy also gravitated towards the Rochester casino in London which wasn't a gambling haunt but rather an entertainment centre which hosted wrestling and roller skating but more importantly for the Ballymoney man it also had on its bill big bands including Count Basie, the Ted Heath Orchestra, Eric Delaney, Joe Loss and Humphrey Littleton, as well as up and coming pop stars like Tommy Steele, Adam Faith and Marty Wilde.

Another visit to London at Easter 1957 proved to be eventful, for all sorts of reasons. Billy and his friend Hubert Dunlop who hadn't booked accommodation found every hotel and guest house were full.

Dressed in brand new Teddy Boy suits they eventually struck lucky at a big hotel called the Roebuck near Buckingham Palace. They were so tired after seeing the sights of London on foot they gladly accepted the offer of the hotel's offer of single rooms which at around £20 cost almost a week's wages.

At breakfast Billy and Hubert were shocked to see the rest of the guests, formally dressed in morning suits and bow ties, staring at them in their Teddy Boy gear and they left without eating.

Their next destination of Soho was even more embarrassing because they were propositioned by 'working girls' whose advances they rejected.

"We got a cheaper hotel in the Strand area which was in the theatre district and we saw a poster for the Lyceum ballroom," says Billy who had seen the ballroom when he watched Come Dancing on television. "At the Lyceum we weren't dressed out of place and we started jiving with some girls (one of whom was from Belfast). We were attracting a lot of attention from other dancers who clapped us. But as we did the Charleston, one of my favourite dances, two bouncers stopped us and pointed out 'no jiving on either side of the stage,' signs which we hadn't noticed.

"The next morning after a visit to the famous Petticoat Lane market we were back on the train to Rochester." On one occasion Billy and one of his dance partners Brenda Cummings who had gone to the Lyceum with friends were seen on TV dancing and his work colleagues were mightily impressed.

One of Billy's lasting memories of a rock and roll competition on Come Dancing that night was a couple from Belfast who were among the pacesetters but the girl burst out of her hot pants and unsurprisingly she had to withdraw. He also recalls that the interval act was the singer Frankie Vaughan who performed his famous high-kicking routine as he sang his hits like Green Door, Give Me the Moonlight and Give Me the Girl.

Other expeditions in England took Billy and his widening circle of friends that included a cousin of Northern Ireland World Cup hero Peter McParland, to all sorts of places including a fun fair where a pal volunteered to take on a boxing challenge in a marquee.

Billy courted one of the dancing friends, Christine Bannfield, the daughter of a Christian missionary in India

However, while they were going out together Billy and Christine encountered problems with a Welsh rugby playing friend of her father's. The man proclaimed himself to be Christine's 'guardian' and started to preach to her and Billy about going to London which he called 'the devil's playground.'

Billy prefers not to name the man who sent him threatening letters with messages like 'And a hand came from the wilderness.' But it got so serious that Billy took the correspondence to the police and the writer ended up in hospital, diagnosed with manic-depression.

"We never heard from him again," says Billy whose relationship with Christine ended in 1959 and with the work coming to an end at the Isle of Grain he returned home in March 1960 to Ballymoney where his mother was ailing but glad to see him in her new home in 15 Armstrong Drive, Glebeside where he had his own bedroom. Billy had become friendly for a time with a girl from County Down, Nora O'Hare, a one-time winner of the Miss Newry title and dancing was again high on the agenda

At one dance in Ballymena the irrepressible Brendan Bowyer from the Royal Showband bounded off the stage and asked Billy where he had bought his suit.

He opened the jacket and showed him the label which read Simpsons of Chatham High Street, a private tailoring company. It was a suit with a distinctive red lining that was to play a significant part in the later life of Billy who was to see Brendan Bowyer again – in Las Vegas and Londonderry.

Billy was delighted to learn that his good friend Ross Fleming was also back home after working in Scotland and the two pals got night shift work in the Braid Water Spinning Mill in Ballymena where the wages were poor. But Billy used his savings to buy a 250cc BSA star motorbike and one snowy night he came a cropper though he wasn't hurt only to discover that Ross was lying uninjured in a hedge too.

Billy applied for a post with a construction company building the new Chemstrand man-made fibre plant in Coleraine but he was deemed too small for the job even though he was taller than Ross Fleming who did obtain a job.

Billy however found work at the Fison's firm which was nearer his home and the pay was better.

Now happier than ever he started going to more dances with a friend called Tony O'Connor (not to be confused with an estate agent Tony O'Connor who featured prominently in Billy's life) and at one of these dances in Ballymoney Town Hall another relationship developed with a girl that Billy used to work with at Balnamore.

However it was a short-lived friendship because the girl's parents banned her from going out with Billy because he was a Roman Catholic.

It wouldn't be the last time that the religious divisions of Northern Ireland would present problems for Billy and his romantic interests.

Uncle James and Granny Lizzie Ramsey, N.A, Sister Ruby, N.A.

4

Forbidden love

He didn't know it at the time but Billy's life was to change forever on Thursday, May 19, 1960. He thought passing his driving test on his motorcycle in Ballymoney that day was reason enough to celebrate but later on at the Arcadia Ballroom in Portrush he met the love of his life. He'd gone on his own to the Arcadia to hear the ever-popular Dave Glover Showband. And he felt like a million dollars in a trendy new suit in the ballroom which was even busier than usual because it was the start of the North West 200 motorbike weekend that brought thousands of people to the north coast.

Halfway through the night Billy who was having a glass of orange on the Arcadia balcony spied an attractive girl with reddish hair who was wearing a flared red / white dress and

The Arcadia Ballroom 1970

33

who was jiving with a local man. Billy didn't hang about. He quickly made his move after the girl sat down and the Showband started to play their next jive number.

Says Billy: "I made a beeline for the girl and politely asked her to dance. We jived under the balcony where most jivers jived, not interfering with the more formal ballroom dancers. We jived together for the rest of the night until the dance was over at around 1am."

The girl told Billy she was Lily Staddon from Armagh and that she was now based outside Portrush.

Ever the gentleman and seizing his opportunity Billy offered to leave Lily home on his motorbike to a bungalow called Summerville that her parents were renting at 32, Ballyreagh Road between Portrush and Portstewart.

Lily didn't want to wake her mother and father and produced a key to a small touring caravan parked nearby where she tried to dry Billy's sweat-soaked jacket and shirt which had turned bright pink because the dye inside had run.

Suddenly there was a knock on the door and a woman who turned out to be Lily's mother Sally demanded to know who was in the caravan with her daughter and forcefully reminded her that she had to be up early the next morning for her work.

Billy left after putting on the protective clothes from his motorbike panniers. But first he arranged to meet Lily again at the Diamond in Coleraine.

Looking back Billy who went on to build up a lucrative caravan business in Northern Ireland smiles at the recollection that his first night meeting Lily, who was to become his wife, was also the first time he had ever set foot in a caravan.

The first date was arranged for 10 days' time – a Sunday - at 7pm. And on that evening after a day out on the North Coast with his friends Ross and Tony on their motorbikes Billy duly headed off to meet Lily in Coleraine. However he thought they'd agreed to meet up at 7.30pm and when he arrived at the Diamond there was no sign of his date.

"I thought Lily had stood me up and I went home, thinking our short romance was over," says Billy. "But on the following Saturday night I bumped into her again at another dance and she explained that she'd had to work late in Ratheane Hospital in Coleraine on the evening that we were due to meet and sent a friend to explain the situation to me. But because I was late her pal gave up."

With the mix-up out of the way Billy and Lily talked and danced, sowing the seeds of an enduring relationship. Ironically the big hit song of the day was to prove rather appropriate – it was Elvis Presley's song Stuck on You!

Says Billy: "Lily who was 18 and I became like two peas in a pod, we were never away from each other except when we were at work. Lily told me she'd come to Portrush because her father Harry Staddon who was a hospital boiler-man in Armagh had transferred to Coleraine. He was a real Cockney, a lovely gentleman who was born within the sound of Bow Bells in London. He and the rest of his family made me feel very welcome and I was very grateful to them.

Lily in the dress she wore when they first met

Lily's mum and dad

Lily's cousin Dick Jones, Lily's brother Dennis & cousin Bernie

Harry Staddon

My sister Elizabeth, brother Hughie, Anne & Sheila Mulholland

Lily aged 14

Lily with grandmother

Armagh Primary School   Lily front row Left-Right 5th girl

"While Lily worked in Ratheane hospital her mother Sally had a job in Hopefield hospital. Her younger brother Dennis was still at school. An uncle who was a mechanic came to live with them but I didn't warm to him at all. He drank a lot," says Billy. "Lily and I enjoyed our time together; we loved going out on the motor bike, and there was the occasional picnic at places like Dunseverick plus visits to the cinema."

Things were changing for the better on the North Coast particularly between Portrush and Portstewart around Ballyreagh which had once been full of dilapidated caravans, old wooden huts, railway carriages, buses and tin shacks. The local council cleared the area and built a housing development in Portrush at Glenmanus as well as vesting land to develop Carrick Dhu and Juniper Hill caravan parks.

After three months going out with Lily, Billy discovered a surprising fact about her father Harry; that he had lost a leg during World War Two. He says:"Harry never talked about the war. Harry met Sally in Armagh when he was preparing troops for the Normandy landings. He was an extremely fit man who trained members of Coleraine Boxing Club and the Boys Brigade in Bushmills."

He also used to train Lily who, like her dad, was a strong swimmer and a fine runner. Indeed Lily once competed on the track against a future Olympic Gold Medal winner, Mary Peters and she also played hockey for Armagh. Dancing was ever present on the social calendar for Billy and Lily and the Arcadia was their number one haunt. One night after they showed their prowess on the dance floor in front of an appreciative crowd the manager handed them an envelope which contained two admission tickets for life to the Arcadia.

"We were delighted and we saved a lot of money going to special nights when the likes of Bill Haley and the Comets, Roy Orbison, the Electric Light Orchestra and the New Vaudeville Band, were playing. And if we weren't working we would dance from 3pm to 5 pm on a Saturday and return again at night to dance some more!"

The big names weren't confined to Portrush, however. Billy recalls going to The Top Hat ballroom in neighbouring Portstewart and paying the £1 entrance fee to hear Acker Bilk and his Paramount Jazz Band who had a surprise in store for their fan.

Says Billy:" Acker Bilk was signing autographs and other members of the band were selling tapes at the end of the night. The musicians recognised me from the Co-op Jazz Club Gravesend. I asked Acker why it was £1 for admittance when it was only two shillings in Gravesend. He replied with a laugh that their hotel, the Carrick-na-Cule in Portstewart was very expensive.

"Lily and I were huge fans of Acker Bilk and loved his clarinet playing on tunes like Stranger on the Shore. We were lucky enough to see him again much later on at the Derry Jazz Festival."

Another star at the Top Hat was Eddie Calvert who played his worldwide hit, Oh Mein Papa, a particular favourite with Billy who had once lingered so long at a dance in Maidstone, Kent to hear it that he missed his train and had to walk the 12 miles home.

In Portstewart another tune that Calvert started to play didn't go down quite so well with most people in the audience. After Eddie struck up with Kevin Barry he was informed that it was an Irish rebel song and he stopped playing it immediately and apologised.

Near the end of August Billy was on the move again. After Fison's he went for a job as a painter on radio masts in the townland of Billy near Bushmills. But it was almost the end of him.

For on his way to the interview a car which was coming out of a T-junction appeared to stop and Billy's motorbike hit the side of it at 40mph.

He says: "I flew over the car and I could see the tarmac coming towards my face. Fortunately I was wearing a fairly new type of crash helmet that covered my ears but when I landed I could feel a pain in my right leg which had gone into an L-shape and my tibia and fibia were shattered."

"When the ambulance came one of the paramedics recognised me as the guy who was going out with Harry Staddon's daughter and he told me 'you won't be dancing for a while now.'

"I remembered that I had been due to meet Lily again outside Ratheane hospital and the ambulance driver swung by and let her into the back of the vehicle on its way to another hospital where I was for six weeks after my leg was set in plaster.

"My mother was very upset but I told her it would have been worse if Lily had been on the pillion behind me. But by serendipity I was transferred to Ratheane hospital to Lily's ward and she looked after me well for another fortnight.

"During my hospitalisation I read my first ever book which ironically given why I was laid up was The Devil Rides Out by Dennis Wheatley. After I got out of hospital Tony drove me and Lily around in a new car he had bought, a Riley soft hood. Later in court the driver of the car involved in my accident was acquitted of a charge of careless driving.

"Lily's family moved to a house at Gortnee near Bushmills and she got a new job in the nearby Runkerry nursing home. After I got used to crutches I would take the bus to visit Lily or sometimes she came to see me. Lily who later acquired a scooter, was frequently extremely busy and had to cope with a flu epidemic during which four residents of the home died."

As Christmas 1960 approached Billy's beloved mother Jeannie was ill and her diabetes got worse, so much so that she was admitted to the Royal Victoria Hospital in Belfast.

Billy visited his mum as often as he could but on December 30 she passed away, leaving him and the rest of his family heart-broken.

He recalls the day of her funeral, on January 1, 1961 as if it were only yesterday. "It was cold and there was snow on the ground. I was still on my crutches and it was a very sad day for all of mum's children who knew she loved every one of us equally. She was only 59 and she is still very much missed, " says Billy who adds that the wake in Armstrong Drive was packed with friends and family who reminisced about his mother and her engaging personality and her 'wee sayings.'

She apparently used to tell people who were annoying her to 'take a salt water walk around a herring barrel' or issue advice that it was 'better to have a small fire that would warm them rather than a big fire that would burn them.' Another favourite was to say that 'no matter how tough a man is he is not a man until he can say thanks and sorry.'

Not long into the New Year Billy feared for the life of his friend Tony who had a bad crash at the Seacon crossing in Ballymoney. His head injuries were so serious that he was anointed by a priest but happily he pulled through.

However Billy was in for an even greater shock after Lily's mother asked to see him in private. The upshot of the conversation was that she told Billy that she didn't want him to see her daughter anymore.

"She said 'you are a Roman Catholic and you will not do well in Northern Ireland.' I countered that I had never been out of work since I left school except for time after breaking my leg. I asked her if Lily who was coming up to her 19th birthday, had any say in the situation but I was told that she would do as her parents instructed her," says Billy "I was a ten and a half stone, pimply faced Teddy Boy who was out of work with a broken leg and on top of all that I was a Roman Catholic in Northern Ireland. I didn't have much going for me."

Billy says he didn't want to cause any trouble for Lily or her family. But the couple were not prepared to accept the parental diktat which they say probably brought them closer together.

And they kept seeing each other. In secret, of course. Lily left her job in the nursing home and started to work in Fison's where Billy, who had bought a new motorbike, was soon to join her.

"We saw more of each other than before, but Lily's mother was getting suspicious. Her so-called 'uncle' Willie was snooping and saw Lily getting off my motorcycle. He made it clear he would tell her mother but Lily said she would acquaint her mum of the fact that Willie had once tried to kiss her. That stopped him in his tracks," says Billy who revealed that Willie had made his feelings about his Catholic religion clear when he told him on one 11th of July to stay away from him the following day, the Twelfth.

The pressure was building on Billy and Lily with their clandestine relationship and after much deliberation they decided there really was nothing to keep them in Northern Ireland and the only alternative was to elope across the water, with Kent or Scotland listed as their two possible options.

They handed in their notice to Fison's and stayed with Billy's sister Jean for two weeks until they set off for Glasgow but they didn't tell anyone where they were heading.

"After we paid our boat fare we counted up that we had £28 between us and all but £8 of that was Lily's," says Billy who laughs as he later insisted to Lily he'd married her for her money!

Lily, Billy and the bike

5

Billy and Lily find a Guardian Angel in Scotland

Billy and Lily arrived in Glasgow with one suitcase each and little in the way of plans for their future. They went to an address off Sauchiehall Street given to Billy by a priest whose nickname was The Sheriff because his surname was Fr Matt Dillon, the same as a fictional character in the TV series Gunsmoke. In Glasgow the Jesuit priest they met offered them a friendly and non-judgmental ear. They told Fr James Francis Langan SJ from St Aloysius Church that they were in Glasgow to find work and to eventually be married. The priest's barrister mother was a member of the Guinness family and his father was a director of the Wimpey construction firm. Fr

The Lacarno Ballroom 1961

Langan offered the O'Neills cigarettes and guidance about accommodation and about the local employment exchange.

He walked his unexpected guests to a nearby sandstone house opposite the city's art college. It was owned by a parishioner called Mrs Cummings in Scotts Street and she said she had two single rooms on separate floors with a shared kitchen, toilet and bathroom available to rent for £4 a week, each.

It wasn't ideal but the eloping couple had little option but to say 'yes' to Mrs. Cummings even though the furniture was 'awful' – Billy fell through a chair and a wardrobe collapsed – but on a brighter note after shopping for groceries they noticed that there was a jazz club called the Cotton Club right next door.

Billy says: "We thought it would be handy for dancing though we weren't sure if the music was going to keep us awake on nights we weren't there but it wasn't too loud."

They also spotted a dance hall in Sauchiehall St called the Locarno. But the first priority was to find work and staff at the employment centre told Billy there was no civil engineering work available.

Instead he accepted a job as a TV aerial store man in premises that were near his new base. He dispatched aerials all around Scotland and with Lily starting work in a bed and breakfast things were looking up. But while Billy wrote to tell his sister Jean he was ok he didn't share the address just in case Lily's parents tried to obtain it from her.

The runaways were content in Glasgow but with no TV in their accommodation they went to the cinema a lot or to the Cotton Club next door or the Locarno Ballroom for the dances.

But Billy and Lily still wanted to be married and Fr Langan SJ told them they would have to live in Scotland for 12 weeks to qualify for a wedding. They picked Saturday, September 23 as their big day at St Aloysius church where Fr Langan SJ agreed to officiate and also to find witnesses.

"I had to obtain a baptism cover note for the ceremony which was to be a mixed marriage. I never asked Lily from that day to this if she wanted to be a Roman Catholic, She had a mind of her own and she wasn't a bit backward about using it," says Billy.

Billy and Lily, who didn't have an engagement ring until many years later, were nervous as the 23rd approached. Billy wore a blue pin-striped suit that he'd got for his sister Elizabeth's wedding to Bob McKee and Lily wore a purple and black outfit topped off by a hat which was lent to her by her landlady Mrs. Cummings who was at the ceremony with her husband. They took pictures but they didn't come out.

The witnesses were John and Agnes Boyle who were teacher friends of Fr Langan SJ who surprised Billy and Lily by telling them he had booked to have dinner for the happy couple, the priest and the Boyles in Glasgow's renowned Grand Central Station Hotel.

Billy and Lily walked to the church where Fr Langan had another nice touch in store, giving the best man a half-crown to set beside the inexpensive wedding ring that the groom had bought for Lily.

Fr. James Langan SJ

Billy recalls: "Fr Langan SJ said 'with this gold ring and silver I thee wed', lovely words we had never heard before instead of 'with this ring I thee wed'

"We had a wonderful meal in the Grand Central. I still remember what we had to eat – honeydew melon, roast beef and pavlova to follow. We all had soft drinks because we were all teetotalers at the time.

"Looking back our very different wedding was so romantic. And that afternoon we went to the cinema, and saw the Nun's Story before we went dancing at the Locarno. The next morning after we went to Mass, we had our first argument, I had about £14 in my pocket and I told Lily I wanted to take her by train to Edinburgh for the day. But she said we would have nothing to live on for the rest of the week and she won the day in the first fall-out of our marriage!

"The next disagreement was with our landlady who still charged us £8 rent even though we were now living in one room, not two but she insisted there were still two people living under her roof!"

To add insult to injury the O'Neills were caught up in a scam in a butcher's shop in Glasgow where an assistant claimed Lily had bought eggs with a £10 note when it was in fact a £20 note. It was a tenner the newly weds could ill afford to lose. The police were called in and it was later discovered that it wasn't the first scam of its kind in the shop and the end result was a court case but not before Billy was called an 'Irish so-and-so'

The secrecy over the wedding was soon ended. Billy wrote to his brother Hughie and sister Jean to tell them that he and Lily had got married.

6

Motoring their way to England and a new arrival

A month after their wedding Billy headed South to England for the commencement of what would turn out to be an exhausting trek up and down the country working on an ever-expanding network of motorways. Billy had received a letter from his brother Hughie in Kent informing that Wimpey had won a contract to build a 12 mile section of the M2 motorway from the River Medway Bridge to the Stockbury Viaduct and they were advertising in the local papers for plant fitters - mechanics to work on heavy earth-moving machinery. It was too good an opportunity to miss, says Billy especially as his brother was offering to let the newly-weds stay with him until they could find a place of their own.

Lily, Billy, Dene O'Neill and Terry O'Neill on his dad's knee

Saying farewell to the priest who they regarded as their friend and a 'guardian angel' was not easy for Billy and Lily and as he left them to the train station he asked them to write to him which they did as well as exchanging Christmas cards until his death in December 2019.

After a long and tiring journey Billy and Lily arrived at Hughie and Joan's house and settled in Billy's old room overlooking the River Medway Bridge

After an interview Billy was employed by Wimpey as a semi-skilled fitter working a 12 hour shift from 7am every morning, Monday to Friday and with overtime he was clearing £30 a week and getting only the occasional Sunday off.

"Working on heavy earth machinery was my main job in Kent. Once the top soil was moved there was chalk underneath and that could be sore on the eyes. As 1961 was coming to an end there was a lot of snow so instead of moving earth we were moving snow and many of the machines were damaged," says Billy who travelled to work on the bus before investing £1.10shilling in a second hand bicycle – a ladies' one – that cut the journey significantly and saved him money.

In March 1962 Billy pedalled home even faster than usual after being told that Lily was about to give birth and on his arrival at the house he saw paramedics leading Joan to the ambulance.

But a smiling Lily informed them that she, and not Joan, was the mum-to-be and she was rushed to All Saints Hospital in Gillingham where a couple of days later she gave birth to a baby boy.

Billy was every inch the proud dad when he saw his son.

Billy's first four wheels - a GPO Morris 8

First Home 18ft Blue Bird caravan

"I thought he was like Lily's brother Dennis and had the Staddon nose but he looked lovely with plenty of the O'Neills dark hair," says Billy who had bought a white wicker crib for the new arrival. It was almost a week before they were allowed home and during that time Billy and Lily discussed names.

He proposed James Francis as a tribute to Fr Langan and while Lily agreed she also liked the name Terry after a high-profile photographer of the day, Terry O'Neill.

In the end they settled for Terry James Francis O'Neill and everyone was happy.

Several months later another important arrival came into Billy's life. After buying himself a new car – actually it was a former Post Office van – the man who would build himself a caravan business was offered his first caravan to buy.

The Mayo man who was selling it told Billy he was moving it on because his father had died. The two Irishmen shook hands on a price of £45 for the 18ft Blue Bird and Billy couldn't wait to share the news of his purchase which pleased Lily but disappointed Hughie who didn't want his house guests to leave, especially to live in a caravan.

But leave they did and Billy borrowed a Land Rover to move the caravan not far from his work to a chicken farm on the splendidly named Robin Hood Lane.

The light blue-coloured caravan needed refurbishment, a task that Billy threw himself into with gusto, working a couple of hours every evening to make it habitable for his family though he once mistook a bottle of paint thinners for the soda he wanted to drink and quickly realised that that was not a good idea.

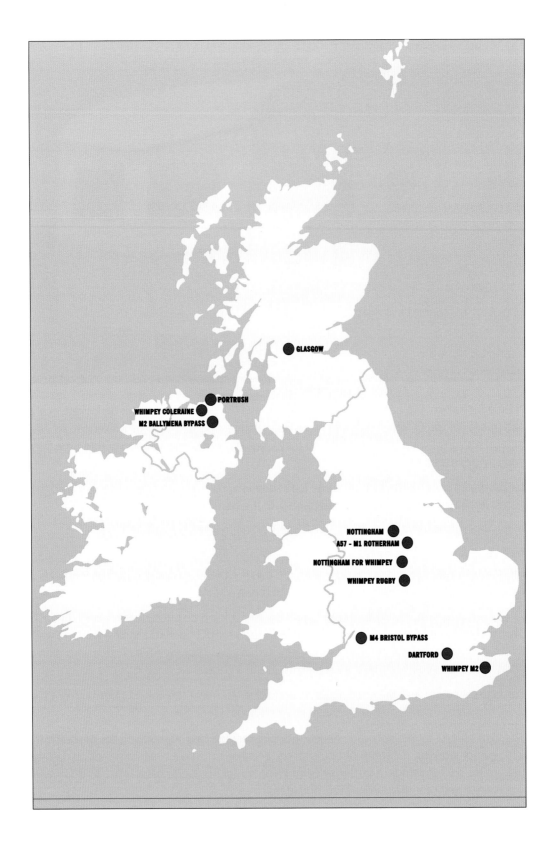

GLASGOW

PORTRUSH

WHIMPEY COLERAINE

M2 BALLYMENA BYPASS

NOTTINGHAM

A57 - M1 ROTHERHAM

NOTTINGHAM FOR WHIMPEY

WHIMPEY RUGBY

M4 BRISTOL BYPASS

DARTFORD

WHIMPEY M2

But no real damage was done and Billy and Lily settled in well in the caravan along with baby Terry and they liked the friendly chicken farmer and his wife who sold them eggs at excellent prices.

Not only was Billy able to see brother Hughie, Joan and their two children but another sibling James and his wife were also based nearby while brother Jack and his family were in Hatfield in Hertfordshire.

Hughie and Joan were also able to babysit Terry to give Billy and Lily their first night out in months. And unsurprisingly they headed for a dance hall..

The somewhat eccentric pop star – and future politician – Screaming Lord Sutch was topping the bill at the Invicta Ballroom in Chatham where part of his 'act' was emerging from a coffin.

Lily quickly found an affinity with Kent and took delight in going for walks with Terry in a brand new pram that she and Billy had bought in the shape of a Vauxhall car of all things.

Billy was trusted to utilise his fitters' skills on a number of projects at work and sometimes toiled on 24 hour shifts that made Lily worry about him.

Another fitter with whom Billy became friendly was Jim Tweed from Southend-on-Sea who had worked on submarines during WW2. Billy says he learnt a lot from Jim and the pair of them used to go for drives in the country on their days off, taking time to look at caravan parks and caravans which were up for sale.

At a residential mobile home park in Rainham in September a 22ft x 8ft Nene Valley Palace five berth caravan, priced £350, caught Billy's eye. It had plenty of bedroom space with the potential for Terry to have a room of his own.

With Billy and Lily's first wedding anniversary approaching it seemed like the perfect present for them to purchase and they traded in their Blue Bird and took out HP to seal the deal. "We were on cloud 9," says Billy who had to move location on the farmer's land.

"The new caravan had a corner chemical toilet but we didn't need it as we had a toilet outside. I turned the indoor facility into a larder and for heat we had a solid fuel fire which kept the caravan warm and cosy. Around that time a colleague Stan Briggs bought himself a 12 bore shotgun that he licensed and he used to shoot the odd pheasant or partridge in the orchards that the M2 was going through. One day I shot a partridge but Stan said I wasted a cartridge because I was so close I could have beaten it to death with the butt of the weapon," laughs Billy who says that the formerly strained relationships with families back home were easing.

"Lily had been in touch with her mother in Bushmills and her aunt Noelle who was back

from overseas with her husband Norman, a Scots born soldier who was working for the Territorial Army in Armagh. They asked to come to visit and to see Terry. Lily was excited to meet up with everyone especially her mother who stayed for over a week. She was curious about whether or not we intended to come home and I repeated what she had once said to me about Roman Catholics not getting on in Northern Ireland and I told her we intended to stay as long as Wimpey needed me.

"I had the weekend off and took Lily, her mother and Terry to see Granny Staddon who had re-married and was living in Brentwood in Essex. She was over 80 and still smoking and she was concerned as to whether or not I had noticed she was wearing a hearing aid."

A few days later Billy was leaving his mother in law Sally – whom he called mum – back to Heathrow airport in his old Post Office van when the family had a lucky escape in a crash.

It was early in the morning and on a foggy country road near Epsom a Rover 90 came out of nowhere and ran into the left hand side of the vehicle, almost toppling it over.

Billy quickly established that everyone was alright and to his amazement he discovered that Terry had actually slept through it all.

"The driver of the Rover was a posh-sounding man and I could smell drink off him. He could see the damage to the side of the van and asked how much it would take to repair it. I knew I could push the dents out and fix the mudguard but I told him I would need £20 for the repairs and he handed me the cash there and then. We were lucky and so was the driver, "says Billy who continued to work on the M2 contract which now involved reconditioning earth movers and other machinery in Wimpey's main depot in Southhall where he and a number of colleagues would work from Monday to Friday, staying in digs. Billy who had changed his Morris 8 van for a Ford 8 Thames van was now a fully paid fitter.

The team were then asked to work in Rugby where Wimpey had won the contract to construct a 20 mile stretch of the M1 from Crick to Leicester.

For Billy and Lily that meant finding a new place to pitch their caravan near the workshop in the village of Swinford (not the Irish one!) and they discovered a farm house in South Kilworth with a large garden. It looked perfect and had a post office and shop just across the street.

A £5 weekly rent, with a sixpence per unit price for the electricity was agreed upon and Billy went back to Robin Hood Lane to tell Lily the good news.

"But she had news of her own," says Billy. "She said she was expecting another baby and we were both delighted. After the caravan was re-located we moved up to South Kilworth and I pushed ahead with the work there. But the weather was cold, so cold in fact that when I was bolting steel beams together a spanner once stuck to my hand."

7

Touching down in Rugby

Billy and Lily's new base was close to the busy town of Rugby where they did their weekly shop and the city of Leicester and the village of Market Harborough were also nearby. With the weather improving Billy and his colleagues were able to start moving earth again but the hours were long and taxing. On his odd days off Billy who had passed his driving test took Lily and Terry on sightseeing excursions to museums and the like. Also on the itinerary were Warwick Castle and Shakespeare's birthplace of Stratford-upon-Avon where the family went on a barge trip before visiting the Bard's famous theatre.

In April Billy's brother Eddie who was out of work, got a job with Wimpey in the concrete batching plant among other places and moved into the South Kilworth caravan.

Great Step Grandson Harris Alexander McGrath

But Eddie was soon on his way back home after he was offered a full-time job with Nestles in Northern Ireland. Billy missed his brother but he was soon welcoming another addition to his family.

On Sunday, August 25, 1963 Lily woke Billy and told him to call an ambulance which went to North Kilworth by mistake and was an hour late getting to Lily but an apologetic paramedic tried to re-assure the O'Neills that he had experience of delivering babies in his ambulance.

"However Lily pleaded with me to take her to the Ashby Magna Hospital and that's where we went, and our new baby son was born within the hour, a brother for Terry who was 17 months old, says Billy. "We had decided if it was a boy we would call him Stephen after an uncle who lived in Portstewart. The new arrival looked just like his grandfather Harry Staddon.

"We lived in South Kilworth for about two years and then we moved the caravan to Dunton Bassett a village between Leicester and Lutterworth. We parked the caravan in a builder's yard and within a few weeks there were six more on site. The owner John Greenough was delighted with the extra income.

"I continued to work for Wimpey who won a contract for the section of the M1 to Loughborough. During the dreadful winter of 1963/4 I was employed in the Lancaster Road, London depot, dismantling and rebuilding Caterpillar earth moving machines. I travelled down on my own in the Thames van on Mondays, stayed in a B & B for four nights and then travelled back to Dunton Bassett on Fridays."

Billy's introduction to his new digs was not an auspicious one. He didn't like the look of the place and locked his suitcase and wallet in his van. Which was just as well because he was awakened on his first night to find a man in his room, stealing his trousers.

Billy gave chase and the thief threw the trousers away after discovering there was nothing in them of any value. The next day, unsurprisingly, Billy decided it was time to move and he went to stay in a guest house in Hillingdon which had been recommended to him.

The elderly couple there, Patrick and Mary Byrne from Kerry, welcomed Billy with open arms and cooked him what he says was good wholesome Irish food for breakfast and dinner.

Billy considered re-locating the caravan down to a site that he had seen near his work but he had second thoughts, mainly due to exorbitant charges and demands, which made him stay where he was.

At Christmas the Byrnes agreed that Billy could bring his family down for a week and said they would look after the children while mum and dad took themselves out for the night.

It almost goes without saying that the destination of choice for the O'Neills was somewhere they could dance and they headed for the Hammersmith Palais where the legendary Joe Loss and his Orchestra were playing.

"We realised we hadn't lost our touch on the dance floor," says Billy who welcomed the arrival of Spring and the news that Wimpey had won yet another contract for the construction of a further stretch of the M1 from Long Eaton to Sheffield.

That necessitated yet another move for the O'Neills and Billy searched out a new site for the caravan with water and electricity supplies outside the town of Sandiacre in the East Midlands. This time a fee was agreed and the location suited the family perfectly because there were plenty of shops and other business premises that Lily could walk to.

The work on the new contract was hard, with lots of earth to move, ensuring that Billy had to work 12 hour shifts. But one day Billy found out just how small a world it really is. As he worked on a Caterpillar D9 he discovered a wallet under the driver's seat and inside was what he estimated from a cursory glance to be around £300.

But there was also a Northern Ireland driving licence registered to a Charlie Green from Macfin, Ballymoney and to his amazement Billy remembered that he had gone to school with him.

A grateful Charlie called with the O'Neills and invited them to dinner in Nottingham along with his brothers Joe and Lawrence who were also working on the M1 contract.

"Lily looked after the children while I went out and the four of us reminisced about school and about dancing. It then emerged that the lads were living in a caravan just a quarter of a mile from ours, " says Billy who was disappointed to learn that he was to be transferred back to London for the winter but he decided that the long journey from Nottingham to the capital was 'not on' and he stopped working for Wimpey in November 1964.

Fate was on Billy's side, however, and he heard from his brother Hughie that the A2 in Kent was being turned into a section of the M2 from Swanscombe to the River Medway. "I knew the area well and I liked Kent. So I made enquiries and found out a firm called Dick Hampton (Earth Moving) had the contract to move the earth so I phoned their office in Alton, Hampshire and I was told to start with them from November 9.

"I was informed the office/workshop for the contract was an old disused Army camp at the Tollgate on the A2 which I knew well so I had the caravan moved down there and got it placed against an old wall of the barracks to protect us from the wind," says Billy who was re-united with some old friends from previous jobs including Ken Orem, Peter Flack and Stan Briggs who were living locally.

There was no let-up for Billy workwise as he turned his hand to maintaining or repairing earth moving machines that had mostly been built before WW2 to level ground in order to build airfields.

Says Billy: "They had what were known as donkey engines which were started by hand cranks and then they started the Caterpillar D8R main engine. I had the machines sitting ticking over for the drivers to begin work at 7am. Turning an existing road into a motorway was more hazardous than creating a motorway on virgin land. Houses had to be removed; bridges had to be re-built and there were a lot of diversions as the A2 was the main road

53

from London to the southern seaside resorts of Margate, Ramsgate, Faversham, Herne Bay, Whitstable and Canterbury."

"All the traffic had to go over a two-way steel bridge in Rochester and loads of vehicles used to boil up sitting in traffic jams on Saturdays and Sundays. Peter Flack came up with the idea of carrying a couple of 5 gallon cans of water to help the vehicle owners out and their tips paid for some of our breakfasts in nearby cafes."

Billy and Lily did their shopping in Gravesend and their sons made friends with other children who were living in the old Army camp which was a fascinating place for Terry and Stephen. Family came calling regularly and there were trips to Brentwood to see Granny Staddon. Billy also bought a new car – a royal blue 1956 Vauxhall Wyvern from a fitter foreman. It was a show car with lots of extra special touches. "I really liked the car. And Lily and the kids were chuffed with it too," says Billy who travelled on a number of occasions to join friends to watch a wrestling contest. "It really was bad acting but it was a night out and one evening I did something else that I had never done before, I drank alcohol. I tried a gin and tonic but it was horrible and I decided to stick with the apple juice."

On another night a giant of a works colleague, a D8 driver with the nickname Big John the Gypsy from the south of Ireland, went with Billy and his friends to see the wrestling where one of the stars on the bill was the infamous star of the 'sport' on television, Mick McManus, who won his fight and responded to the boos and cat-calls by inviting all-comers to take him on.

John the Gypsy who was 6'4" and tipped the scales at 18 stone rose to the challenge but no sooner was in the ring than McManus knocked three of his teeth out with a drop-kick.

Other wrestlers that Billy and his friends saw were Giant Haystacks – later to be seen throwing UTV's Jackie Fullerton to the floor - along with 'Judo' Al Hayes and 'Black Butch' Johnston performing for the crowd.

The wrestling wasn't confined to venues outside the caravans. Near where the O'Neills lived, a young ganger enjoyed bringing young lady-friends home and their amorous adventures could be heard far and wide, disturbing other people's sleep. Indeed the employee was so brazen about his exploits that he put up a sign in the window, saying 'if the van is rocking, don't come knocking.'

Several of his closest neighbours got their own back by waiting until he was actually asleep and then throwing bread on his roof to encourage birds to land and keep HIM awake. It did the trick, according to Billy who took the opportunity of coming home with his family to Northern Ireland for four weeks in the winter of 1965 and stayed with Lily's parents in their new home in Hopefield Avenue Portrush, where Terry and Stephen who had lived in caravans throughout their young lives were intrigued to see an upstairs in a house with beds in it! Billy caught up with family and friends in Ballymoney and also laid a holly wreath on his mother's grave.

No prizes for guessing, of course, that Billy and Lily also fitted in a night's dancing at the Arcadia but their sons didn't settle and cried incessantly while their folks were away.

Tragedy nearly struck that Christmas when on an excursion to Armagh in Billy's Vauxhall car a spring broke on the descent of a snow covered hill on the Newry Road. The car which had seven people in it went into a skid and narrowly avoided crashing into the wall of a house. Everyone inside was shaken but they weren't hurt.

It was during that trip back home that Billy and Lily started thinking seriously about returning to Northern Ireland for good or for at least part of the time. The boys were getting bigger and would soon be going to school so the O'Neills began house hunting and bought 158 Causeway Street in Portrush which was close to St Patrick's church and school and their new home was also close to Lily's parents and her friends Hazel Liken and Doris Ramage not to mention the Arcadia. But in the meantime the O'Neills went back to Kent and Billy was transferred from the M2 contract to the Worksop in Nottinghamshire to work on a new stretch of the M1 to Rotherham.

Again the caravan was off on its travels, this time to a park which had once been used by miners at a coal pit near Kiverton Park which was close to the new section of the motorway. Billy who says Terry and Stephen were amazed to see their home moving again, but were also sad to leave Kent and their friends behind. Sadly one of them, Ken Orem who had been fond of Terry and Stephen took his own life after his wife died of cancer.

After the 190 mile journey to Rotherham Billy who was then 27 parked up in the half-full caravan park and was soon flat out on the new task at hand. Luckily a spin-off for the O'Neills was that the earth that was being moved contained a lot of pure coal which was handy for the solid fuel stove in their caravan.

Lily's brother Dennis and his tiler friend Willie Pollock from Bushmills got jobs on the contract, the former as a fully qualified diesel fitter and the latter as a machine banks man.

A fatal accident on the site deeply upset Billy and his colleagues. A young engineer was pegging out the central reservation when he was crushed under an 8ft wheel of a 657 Caterpillar machine after the driver pretended to scare him. "It was sad and sickening," says Billy. "And it just underlined the fact that mucking around can cause a lot of serious accidents on civil engineering sites."

By the end of the summer Lily and the boys had returned to Portrush so that Terry could start school leaving Billy, Dennis and Willie in the caravan. They were profoundly distressed by the news that 144 children had been killed in October 1966 after a colliery tip collapsed and engulfed their school in Aberfan in Wales.

Demonstrating the Jive

Holiday in Caneria

Edgewater Hotel, Portstewart

Lily ,Terry and Stephen Causeway Street Portrush

8

A bad break for Billy and a return to the port

Billy's concerns about safety on construction sites proved all too real on a personal level after he was seriously injured in an accident on a site on the A57 between Sheffield and Nottingham a year later as work was going on to refit a track to a Caterpillar D8 bulldozer. At the crucial moment a mistake with the steel hook of a crane by the machine's operator meant that the one and a half ton track fell back breaking Billy's tibia and fibia again, a repeat of his injury of August 1960.

At Rotherham hospital a doctor spotted the similar nature of the injury and after establishing that Billy could use crutches discharged him the following day. Billy whose right leg was in plaster cast knew it was going home time and a man who bought his Vauxhall car drove him to the ferry in Stranraer. Of course the caravan went too.

The O'Neills' new house in Causeway Street had been let long term and the family lived in a summer home at the rear. Billy broke the news of his leg break to Lily who had been taking

Caterpillar D8 bulldozer

the boys to school and to St Patrick's church, leading to local people thinking she was a Catholic. Billy took over the school and church run duties but if he thought that his medical problems were over, he was sadly mistaken.

One night he was playing ball with a poodle called Tina that Lily was looking after for her father and the dog suddenly made a lunge with her front paws for Billy, hitting him on his 'good' leg on his thigh.

Billy says: "I shot up like a Jack in a box and the next night in bed I had a pain in my side like someone was sticking a knife into me. Lily panicked and phoned our doctor who was off duty but came to see me. Dr Craig at first thought I had pleurisy until I coughed up blood. He got the ambulance straight away and it transpired I had a clot in the lung from the fracture."

As Christmas approached the O'Neills were able to settle into the main house on Causeway Street after their tenants moved out. Billy was sent home from hospital and had to have a bed set up on the ground floor. "It was good to be back home," he says. But Billy wasn't a man built for idleness, living downstairs in Portrush with a broken leg wasn't for him. Even with his injuries he managed to construct built-in wardrobes in his new bedroom.

Another home improvement was the installation of a full glass inner front door to replace a half glass one. But on his return from school one day Stephen mistook the glass door for an open one and ran right through it, though quite astonishingly he escaped without a scratch.

The boys were in their element in Portrush and the family's 'great neighbours' Mr and Mrs Jack Sinclair took them along with their two boys and a girl to a Sunday school on the beach where they used to give the lessons, a forerunner to a gospel hall that the Sinclairs built nearby.

Stephen's narrow escape left him more cautious but once when he said he was afraid of the dark his brother Terry shouted to him: "Put your trust in the Lord "– a story Billy was to repeat at both sons' weddings some years later.

After Billy's plaster was removed from his leg and following extensive physiotherapy at the Robinson Hospital, Ballymoney he was back on his feet and bought himself a new Ford 8 Thames van.

And it was while he was driving from Portrush to Bushmills on a snowy winter's day that the seeds were sown for a remarkable friendship that was to last a lifetime. Along the road Billy stopped his van to pick up a young honeymooning couple who were thumbing a lift to the Giant's Causeway.

The young man introduced himself as Doyle Raymer from Indiana and said his wife Zaira was from Brazil. He said they were hoping to spend a few days in the youth hostel at Whitepark Bay. "I drove them to the Causeway and waited for them but I thought that the youth hostel might not be open because it was winter. So I offered them the free use of our caravan which was parked at Skerry View and was empty," says Billy. Not surprisingly the newly-weds accepted the invitation and during their time in Portrush a bond developed between them and their hosts, to the extent that the couples exchanged greetings cards and letters over the years.

Billy and Lily return to the Arcadia 1964

And during a visit to America in the 80s the O'Neills visited the Raymers at their home where it transpired that Doyle had joined the American army and served in Vietnam after studying at West Point. After leaving the Army Doyle travelled the world and took time out to visit Billy and Lily who brought him on a nostalgic visit back to the Causeway.

But back in the 60s with Billy's leg improving he got more therapy for his injury in the form of dancing at the Arcadia and with the weather improving, Billy returned to earth moving work in England for Dick Hampton who had won the contract for a new by-pass at Bristol.

The family were sad to see Billy go at the end of May but he bought the kids a pet – a guinea pig whose name proved somewhat problematic. One of the boys wanted to call the guinea pig Petty while the other boy plumped for the name Higgins after his schoolteacher. As a compromise the guinea pig was named Petty Higgins.

In England Billy began looking towards a permanent future back in Northern Ireland and he contacted a firm called C.A. Blackwell Contracts (NI) Ltd, an earth moving firm who promised to contact him when they started work on a by-pass for Ballymena on behalf of Farran's Ltd.

But in the meantime in Bristol Billy got digs with a family who lived near the Clifton Suspension bridge while he and his colleagues cleared the way for part of the M32 which entailed going through a lot of orchards whose apples were used for making Scrumpy dry cider.

Billy enjoyed the entertainment scene in Bristol but he was only in the city for three months before he was transferred to another Dick Hampton contract on what was known as the Golden Valley by-pass on the M5 near Gloucester and Cheltenham whose race course held little fascination for him. He was more intrigued by the fact that Rolls Royce and Bentley cars sold more in Cheltenham than in any other city in England.

Near Christmas in 1967 Billy got the news he'd been hoping for – that Blackwell's had a job for him on the Ballymena by-pass starting in the following January.

The work suited Billy to a tee. He was able to drive up and down to Ballymena from Portrush every day; he got another bit of income from renting out his caravan to a work colleague and he made a number of good friends like Jimmy Vine, Jimmy Crawford, his father Danny and brother Joey.

But again there was tragedy up ahead. A contract agent called Keith Morley who had a wife and young children was killed after a Caterpillar 657 motor scraper he was driving overturned in wet conditions near Gracehill bridge.

In a lighter moment works manager Sammy Woodhead from Yorkshire was injured in a fall down an embankment and when he was asked why he was signing himself out of hospital said he was hungry!

Working on the M2 Billy was able to re-acquaint himself with Ballymena-based members of his O'Neill family including his aunt Maggie Larkin and his uncle Hugh, a prisoner of war during WW2 who had worked on the notorious Burma railway. Another relative, Billy's uncle Tom had died during the First World War.

In Ballymena Billy's cousin Peggy O'Neill was married to Irish international footballer Hubert Barr who played for Ballymena United, Linfield and Coventry City.

On the by-pass contract there was rarely a dull moment for Billy who recalls 'great fellowship' among the workers including Sammy Woodhead who enjoyed playing pranks. Billy also liked a practical joke including one where he used a three foot long steel rule to tilt Jimmy Vine's cap off his head just as earth movers were blasting their way through rock.

"Jimmy who had taken up a position with the rest of us a long way from the explosion said 'Oh my God the blast has blown my cap off," laughs Billy who after the Ballymena job found himself transferred to another Blackwell earth moving contract at Randalstown.

9

Turning a blind eye to intimidation and starting a new career on the coast

The month of August 1969 was a traumatic and difficult time in Northern Ireland, a time when life changed dramatically for everyone who lived there. It was the dawn of the troubles that were to claim over 3,500 lives during decades of conflict. And Billy came face to face with the heightened tensions after he made another move to a job that was even closer to his home. On his second day the new boy found a large Union flag hanging above his toolbox on his work bench. The message was unmistakeable.

Entry to Coleraine Mayor's Show

Doyle, Zaira, Natalia and Floyd Raymer Billy and Lily in Washington DC

Doyle receives award

Stores at Ballyreagh Road - purchased 15th Feb 1971

Lily's family visiting from Armagh 1972

"It was a surprise. However it didn't bother me one bit. None of my family ever bit the hand that fed them. It stayed there for months and months," says Billy who moved his caravan for holiday hire to Margoth (now Skerries) caravan park in Portrush that was owned by the late Sam Henry.

Talking of feeding, Billy's attempts to do the cooking in the O'Neill household had come to a soggy, and sorry, end in July 1969 when the family and other relatives headed south of the border on a camping trip which was ruined by showers that engulfed a borrowed tent that had no ground sheet.

Billy, who had never spent the night in a sleeping bag before, smiles as he recalls that he wasn't dressed for the trip, in a blue pinstriped suit with a white shirt and tie.

In the morning when he offered to cook a fry on a Primus stove under canvas he set a pan down on the plastic wrapping of the bacon and almost smoked everyone out of the tent.

"Lily took over the cooking of breakfast and she has done so ever since," says Billy who was happy working with his new company as they treated their employees well. Billy was eager to please and managed to solve problems that had eluded fitters who had been flown in from England to solve them. He took pride in turning two scrapped Caterpillar D8R bulldozers into one finely turned machine at a fraction of the cost of a new one, a transformation that earned Billy an unheard of £50 bonus from his employers. Another spin-off was that the Union Jack vanished from his work bench because his colleagues were so impressed with him having been given the bonus.

Billy was approached to trouble-shoot on other Caterpillars and the upshot of a series of meetings with his boss Victor Kane, was that he was asked if he would be interested in buying a bungalow and a small shop in Portrush because Victor was thinking of emigrating to Australia.

Without hesitation Billy said 'yes' because the move seemed to tick a number of boxes especially as it would mean a job for Lily at a time when both Terry and Stephen were at school.

Billy remembers the date of his purchase clearly because February 15, 1971 was also the day that decimalisation was introduced in the UK and Ireland.

The bungalow was ideal for the O'Neill family and Billy who was awaiting compensation for his motorbike and industrial accidents some years earlier, sold 158 Causeway Street within a few days of putting it on the market. He was soon taking up a new job as a fitter with Wimpey who had won a contract from the Northern Ireland Housing Trust to build new houses at Harper's Hill in Coleraine.

Billy's workmates wondered if his decision to leave the firm had had anything to do with the Union flag incident and he assured them that there was no connection and that he felt that he had been treated with respect by all his colleagues.

At Harper's Hill Billy was amazed to receive a letter from the Engineering Union to say he wasn't entitled to work as a mechanic because he didn't belong to a trade union but he was able to get proof from the Transport and General Workers Union that he was in fact a card-carrying member and he also got written confirmation from his previous employers that he had worked for them as a mechanic/fitter.

However a completely new era arrived for Billy and Lily when they got the keys for the shop – Ballyreagh Stores - they'd bought at 16 Ballyreagh Road, Portrush. It was a place which already held special memories for them as it was in the shop in their courting days they used to buy their favourite sweets, Cadbury's Lucky Numbers.

But day one wasn't all that lucky for Billy who lost the keys to the shop and had to break a small window in the back door to gain access.

Lily revelled in her new role at the shop and brought any new toys home for Terry or Stephen to try out.

They didn't know it at the time but in the autumn of 1972 the lives of Billy and Lily changed for ever when a man who had a 22ft x 8ft Belmont caravan in the council-owned Carrick Dhu park beside the shop said he wanted to sell it at the end of the summer season instead of putting it in storage for the winter as dictated by the local authority.

Billy was told the asking price was £500 and when a couple inquired about buying it he told them they could have it for £575.

Says Billy: "I thought the seller would give me the £75 above his asking price but how wrong I was. I gave him the £575 in cash and he handed me back a fiver. It was my first 'sale' of a caravan and started me on my way in the caravan business. And that transaction and the fact that I only got a fiver for my trouble was the best lesson I could have ever learnt and after that I charged a percentage on any subsequent sales.

"Eventually Lily took on the agency to sublet and service caravans. We still had our caravan on Margoth which was a big park that had once been two parks Cloughor and Skerryview which were owned by two brothers called Warke.

"I suggested putting a mobile shop on Margoth and after a bit of haggling we agreed on a price. I used our own caravan for the shop. I removed all the doors from the kitchen along with the double wardrobe, the dropdown bed and fitted shelves opposite the entrance door.

"I created a door in and a door out for one customer at a time and I kept the bedroom as a store.Everything worked well. I got the agency to sell the daily and local papers and it was the right time of the year to attend trade shows for toys including seaside toys and souvenirs."

The end of the Harper's Hill contract meant that Billy who had fast become a regular customer at Holmes Cash and Carry outlets was able to become more involved with the Margoth and Ballyreagh shops and eventually he gave up working as a mechanic.

However amid repeated demands for him to pay more rent for the shop at Margoth Billy decided to take the caravan off the site and he used it as a store at Ballyreagh.

But Cedric Dobson from Dobson's caravan park at Glenmanus approached Billy and asked him if he would be interested in renting a shop he was building on his site. Billy re-located the caravan which had been at Margoth to Dobson's until the permanent shop was finished.

But things took a sinister turn in 1972 during a two day strike by loyalist workers, not to be confused with the longer lasting Ulster Workers Council strike two years later.

Billy explains: "Lily was working on her own in the shop at Ballyreagh when about five or six young men came in carrying a large Union Jack and said that she had to shut down, they were also using the flag as a cover for them shoplifting.

"Lily walked to the shop door as if to open it to let them out but instead she locked them in and asked them if they thought stealing behind their flag was loyalism. She picked up the phone and said if they didn't empty their pockets she would call the police and their 'boss.'

"They did as she told them and left but after I returned from delivering gas to Dobson's shop, I could see Lily was upset. She said she'd had a phone call from a man calling himself Captain Black and ordering her to close. Which she did."

Round Table Rally

10

Another new turn for Billy as the caravan rolls on

Billy added a new string to his bow despite the chaos in Northern Ireland. After discovering that some caravan park owners weren't selling their own caravans or earning commission. Cedric Dobson said he had no one to do sales and Billy offered to take on the role after the two men agreed a percentage deal for him. "I contacted the N.I. Dealers saying I was the new salesman for Dobson's Caravan Park and I said I wanted them to supply me with caravans on a sale or return basis. Some were eager to do business and I negotiated a trade discount.

Arcadia Portrush

"Cedric had two sons and a daughter (who was married to Gerry Neill whose mother had just built a caravan park in Ballycastle). By the end of that season I had sold 89 caravans on commission," says Billy who then went out completely on his own to establish an agency which would bring in more caravans from trade shows in Hull where most of them were built.

Competition among dealers at the show which Billy attended in September 1973, was fierce. Some of them were trying to land big orders ahead of Billy to sell caravans into North Coast sites like Carrick Dhu, Juniper Hill and Kelly's.

Billy initially came up against brick wall after brick wall in his attempts to set himself up as an agent for any of the bigger companies in England. Eventually his persistence and patience paid off when Castle Caravans said they would give him the agency for Northern Ireland and he placed an order with them for 12 caravans consisting of one and two bedroom models at 22ft, 26ft and 29ft.

Billy says: "On the way home to Ireland Lily said she'd heard people in Hull talking about a French woman called Madam Du Prey who always ordered at least 2,000 caravans because she was the top distributor in Europe. I told Lily she would have to 'pray' for me that I could sell the 12 caravans I had just ordered."

Sealing the deal was cause for celebration for the O'Neills and they decided to stop in Blackpool where, surprise, surprise, they headed to the legendary Tower Ballroom to dance at an afternoon tea event and in the evening at a big band show.

Another sadder diversion on that journey was to Barrow in Furness where Billy visited his father's grave in a peaceful area overlooking the Irish Sea.

"I took photos of his grave and the house where dad, his brother Tom and other workers from our area lived while they were working replacing roofs on bombed factories. My brother Hughie said that dad had saved up £38 pounds towards starting the ice cream business again but it was never found," says Billy who knew his association with Cedric Dobson would soon come to an end because his sons and daughter were taking an interest in the family business.

Billy's first Castle caravan arrived in the docks and he signed an agreement with a local man John Steel to do all his transporting.

The compensation claims for Billy's accidents which stretched back years still hadn't been resolved and he went to the Law Society regarding his solicitors. The compensation was duly paid and Billy used the money to help pay off his mortgage with Victor Kane for the house at Ballyreagh within just over two years.

The O'Neills struck up a friendship with their next door neighbours Bill and Kate Balmer who were also close to Victor Kane and said they were going to visit him and his family in Australia. Eventually they did make the trip and Lily said she and Billy would go too. "She made it sound as if she was going to Dervock, not down under," says Billy who was encouraged by the interest in his Castle caravans, two of which he sold onto Dobson's park.

Before Christmas he received letters from Ascot and Minister Caravans who had wanted him as an agent for their caravans after previously turning him down at the show in Hull.

But Billy said that space was a problem and that he would contact them when the parks opened up again.

In the meantime he sold three caravans into Donegal, two of them in Kerrykeel and the other one in Portnoo. Another inquiry came from a man who wanted to buy a caravan if he could secure him a plot in a Park at Burnside Road, Portstewart which even Billy didn't know existed.

After tracking down and approaching the owner, a Mrs Katherine Kelly about selling a caravan onto her park, Billy was stunned by what she said next.

For she offered to sell him the caravan park which she said had been on the market for two years.

After a couple of twists and turns Billy finally sealed the deal to buy the park and again to his astonishment Mrs Kelly said she would lend him the money. A commercial mortgage was set up at a favourable rate and Billy was the proud owner of Burnside Caravan Park, his first but by no means his last.

The mortgage was set up by Billy's solicitor Robin Wray from the Wray and Baxter firm.

Burnside Caravan Park 1974

11

A walk in the (caravan) park for Billy

illy could hardly wait to return home to tell Lily the good news that they owned a caravan park and she was chuffed, agreeing with her husband's assertion that someone up above liked them. With the nuts and bolts of the handover completed Billy thought about clearing the park of all old caravans, some of which were made of hardboard while others had felt roofs. One was occupied permanently by the mother of a highly respected local man who wanted her to move in with his family. "I finally made a decision that only caravans built after 1970 could stay on the Park which meant there would be only three left on the Park that had a licence for 75 pitches," says Billy who told the aforementioned lady resident of his plans to modernise the Park and she agreed to live with her son.

Granny Sally with Terry and Stephen

Burnside Holiday Park

Our second home

One man stayed on site. He was called Jack and he was the warden of the park. Billy quickly went about making the caravan park more up-to-date, placing a modern caravan near the entrance to act as a sales office and a space for caravan sales and displays.

Billy then contacted Ascot and Minster Huntsman again who supplied him with some of their caravans.

As time passed Billy was asked about his intentions for the new park by one of three people whose caravans were left on the front row overlooking the golf club. The man, a wealthy businessman, wanted to know if the plan was to sub-let any caravans but Billy said no and that the park would be for private ownership only.

"My reckoning was that sub-letting would only spoil good sales. The businessman said he was pleased to hear that and he insisted he would be staying on," says Billy who tidied up the park and persuaded the roads authorities who were putting a six foot storm drain down Burnside Road to use the hard-core from the trench they were digging to fill in a low-lying area adjacent to the golf course because it improved the look of the place.

"By the end of 1974 I had almost filled the park with new caravans only. And Mrs Kelly asked me if I would be interested in buying a two and a half acre field next to the park. Again I said yes and then I had plans drawn up to extend the park to 99 sites which was eventually reduced to 92 sites to allow for a playground space in the middle of the site.

"I also had a customer who wanted to acquire pitch number 42 which had been levelled off. He said he would buy the biggest caravan available and would pay for a concrete or tarmac base as well as having water and electric fitted at his expense.

"I agreed and phoned George Connell of Orchard Caravans in Belfast and the customer picked up a Donnington Castle 42 foot mobile home from them with a bath and shower which I bought and installed on the Park.

"We took water and electricity from the toilet block and by 1975 I was inundated with requests from the existing pitch customers wanting what I now call full amenities. A surgeon who was on call 24/7 wanted a phone line which I provided. I wrote to all the customers on the park, asking if they wanted full amenities. I said to myself If I reach 51% who want full amenities I will put them into them all and those who don't want them I will leave spurs for the future. Rather than bring in a digger and move the caravans my brother Eddie and his son Paul along with my brother in law Dennis and myself dug all the trenches by spade, pick and shovel. A friend Tony McWilliams then put in the cables with the connections carried out to Northern Ireland Electricity standard.

"However two men in grey suits called with me and told me they were from the Office of Fair Trading (OFT) from Westminster and they questioned me why I wasn't letting people onto my park unless they bought their caravans from me. I explained that I lived in a caravan in England for five years and was unable to rent a site for my caravan while I worked on motorway construction and I asked them why the law here wasn't the same as in England, Scotland and Wales.

Billy insisted he didn't want other dealers to sell caravans onto the park which he had upgraded at a cost of thousands of pounds and he argued that if he didn't have the income from sales he would have to treble or quadruple his rents to cover his investment.

He also said that if he let staff go who were carrying out repairs and services to caravans he would have to call in a dealer from Belfast at substantially higher cost.

"I received a letter from the OFT saying the cure would be worse than the disease," says Billy whose mother-in-law Sally was running the shop at Dobson's caravan park but there were ongoing problems with break-ins and burglaries until a 12 year old boy was caught in the act and to save his own skin gave up the names of fellow culprits who were later apprehended by police and jailed.

David Pudner, Great grand daughter Emily Elizabeth Grace, Grand daughter Arlene Pudner Great Grand Parents Billy & Lily

Aerial view of Edgewater

Aerial view of Castlerock Caravan Park

12

Rocking up to Castlerock

Billy was always on the look-out for fresh ideas and had no hesitation in taking up an offer of acquiring the sales rights onto the York House caravan park in Castlerock from an Englishman called Neil Brierley who had a dental clinic in Coleraine and ran the park as a sideline. Billy also secured a few sales into the local golf club but within a month he got a phone call from a man using the loyalist paramilitary codename of Captain Black who told him to stop selling into Castlerock. The police were informed and Billy went ahead with selling caravans wherever he could and business was booming and not only was he selling caravans from England but he was also buying from main dealers in NI, Orchard for Pemberton Caravans, Moore's for A-Line Caravans and Scott's for Belmont ABI.

Caravan Exhibition Earls Court London

Says Billy: "I was taking orders from sub-agents, who were collecting straight from the docks and I heard of a company in the South of Ireland who made caravans called Rolons. I phoned up and ordered one to be collected the next day. John Steel and I drove down and collected it which turned out was the last caravan they ever produced.

"I put the Rolon on display beside the shop at Ballyreagh where a lady called Mrs Alexander viewed it and bought it for a pitch she had acquired just behind the shop. The woman was the spitting image of Margaret Thatcher so the story went about that I had sold the Prime Minister the Rolon!" Within two years Billy was the agent for an ever-growing number of caravan firms - Atlas, Aztec, Ascot, Castle, Minster Huntsman, Majestic, Mardon, Marfleet, Sovereign and Stately Mobile Homes Ltd, Wales, as well as Majestic and Cumbria,

"I had sales onto ten parks and had 14 sub dealerships but I needed more space for storage so I used the field for which planning had been applied. I thought I wouldn't be breaking any law as there was no-one living in any of the caravans but within a few weeks a planning officer called at the park, with a letter demanding the removal of the caravans forthwith, " says Billy who complied with the order.

Not long afterwards he was visited by Sam Henry who knew the O'Neill family well and he told him that if his mother was still alive she would be proud of him and what he had achieved with his caravan business but he warned him that 'there will be people who will be tramping on your toes.' Billy replied that it had already started. More problems with the planning authorities followed. And on one occasion Billy was told that he didn't have permission for a mobile home on a site, a claim which he disputed.

The owner of the mobile home contacted the local MP the Rev Ian Paisley, the leader of the Democratic Unionist Party who was able to back up Billy's assertion about the planning permission. The mobile home stayed where it was.

Regarding Billy's application for planning for his two and a half acre extension to the Burnside Park a public meeting was held in a room in Coleraine Town Hall where the leading barrister Desmond Boal QC represented him.

However after an at times heated meeting where a number of objectors opposed the extension Billy lost the application on the grounds that the land was zoned for housing development.

But the setback didn't stop Billy who managed to acquire freehold on more land which he needed for sales and storage and after a protracted and unsuccessful attempt to buy land in Portstewart he realised that his brother Davy was spot on when he used to say that 'if something's for you it won't go past you'

Proof of that particular pudding came when Billy got a phone call from Neil Brierley asking if he would be interested in buying his caravan park in Castlerock because he and his family were moving back to Yorkshire.

Billy swiftly answered in the affirmative and Neil told him that there was already an offer on the park which consisted of 14 acres with planning permission for 250 static caravans.

Neil said he would sell Billy the park if he would match the existing offer which he did.

Billy formally took over the park on July 1, 1976 and kept the warden, Joe Makin, on to manage it until his retirement. Joe was also the man who came up with the name Bonalston Lady for a Doberman pup which Billy had bought. The name came from the initials of Billy O'Neill and Lily, Stephen and Terry O'Neill.

Billy still leaves a wreath on the graves of Joe and his wife Hilda every Christmas plus another floral tribute at the final resting place of Mrs Kelly just eight plots away.

More and more Billy found himself unhappy with a number of elements in the planning processes in Northern Ireland and how it seemed to him that a number of caravan sales were operating without official permission. He arranged a meeting with the head of the planning service in the County Hall and after a lot of to-ing and fro-ing and the mention of the Rev Ian Paisley's concerns plus the revelation that Billy would have to sack eight of his workers, there was an about-turn on a decision to refuse him planning permission for a sales yard on a site at Cashlandoo near Portstewart.

Billy had challenged the original rejection which the planners had said was based on the fact that his new development would be a road hazard. Billy produced photographs of some unlicensed parks – and one which did have planning approval - which he said presented more real traffic problems than his proposed site.

Afterwards with the profits of a property sale Billy set about making improvements to his newly named Castlerock Holiday Park and paying for full amenities to be added to the Burnside Holiday Park.

In September 1976 Billy and Lily returned to the caravan trade show in Hull where things happened fast. On the very first night after dinner Rosemary Lane the sales manager of the prestigious A Line group of caravans and her boss David Wilkinson asked Billy how many caravans he would order if he was offered the main dealership for the company in Northern Ireland. He said he would order 400 different models and he was soon told he'd got the contract and he took another 40 caravans as well.

But Billy didn't stop there. He ordered dozens more caravans from other companies.

The caravans arrived over a 12 month period from September 1976 with Lily's brother Dennis driving up and down to Larne harbour, sometimes twice a day, to take delivery of them.

Billy who'd appointed a sub-agent in Limerick sold 200 caravans that year and his driver was taking them south of the border often twice a week on the O'Neills' lorry transporter.

Not everything went smoothly however. And the Garda Siochana were called by Billy who reported the theft of five caravans which he'd arranged to sell to a man in Dublin. The caravans were later found and sold on to another customer but the original client was never heard of again.

Billy later won a legal action after a claim over the ownership of one of his parks by a relation of the previous owner Mr Kelly who said he had been left it in a will.

Says Billy: "After the upgrades to the Burnside park were complete one family of caravan owners who had left the site said they would like to move back because they missed their friends who had stayed. And I was able to secure them the first row pitch available.

Other former caravan owners came back too after the enjoyment of owning a static caravan. Some of the longer term caravanners have been at Burnside for 47 years and the owners included a permanent secretary in the Northern Ireland Office, a leading official in world rugby and several people with knighthoods.

Northern Ireland Hoteliers with Prince Charles on the Royal Yacht Britannia

13

Unfounded rumours, Royal invites, winning awards and meeting Fred Astaire

n May 1977 Billy was told a substantial house at 36 Ballyreagh Road Portrush, with two acres of flat land beside it was going up for sale. And he immediately thought it would make a perfect road front for caravan sales beside the Carrick Dhu and Juniper Hill parks which were owned by the local council and whose owners often came to the O'Neills if they needed repairs.

The Royal Yacht Britannia

Fred Astair and Ginger Rogers

The house and land which had belonged to a local doctor came up for auction in an office in New Row in Coleraine and Billy eventually outbid the other interested parties and regarded his purchase as a good buy.

In July Billy moved from 16 Ballyreagh Rd to 36 Ballyreagh Road and the extra space was invaluable with four large bedrooms, a large reception room and a dining room overlooking the sea.

But Billy was in for a pleasant surprise after spending the first night in number 36 waking up in a curtain-less room to see police and people everywhere outside, not to mention the Royal Yacht Britannia which had brought the Queen and the Duke of Edinburgh on a visit to the University of Ulster at Coleraine. There were so many cars outside the O'Neills' new home that they told the Police the drivers were welcome to park on the lawn.

In November 1977 Billy was preparing to go to London for the Earl's Court caravan show when he learnt about a massive opportunity to buy land that was up for sale nearer home.

Billy told a friend that he didn't even know Reid's 27 acre farm in Mill Road, Portstewart was on the market because it wasn't a road he used very much. But he made a point of arranging a viewing and set the wheels in motion to buy it. He recruited a friend to make the inquiries about it and later to buy it at auction at a time when Billy let his competitors know that he would be in London, making them think he wasn't in the running for the land.

The ploy worked and the bid from Billy's man for the Mill Road land was successful. Another piece of the O'Neill jigsaw was in place.

But Billy's application for planning permission at 36 Ballyreagh Road which he saw as ideal for caravan sales was turned down in successive years, 1977, 1978 and 1979.

Billy was not a happy man and his mood darkened even further after a friend who was involved in the world of finance told him that there were rumours circulating about where he was getting the money to fund his operations.

The friend told him he knew the money was coming from the UDT, Forward Trust and from the Northern Bank.

But within a week Billy's Northern Bank manager asked him to come to his office for a meeting which he thought would be about a charity with which they were both associated.

However the manager said he was embarrassed to report that his superiors had asked him to reconcile Billy's lodgements with his invoice books.

Billy settled himself down for a long meeting at which he assured the bank manager that he kept scrupulous records of all his transactions which he was confident would put an end to all the rumours.

He told the manager that he was doing business with clergymen, police officers, doctors, solicitors, school teachers and even bank managers.

All the while Billy was still having planning permission applications rejected, one for a road house or a licensed inn at 16 Ballyreagh Road;

Millfield Holiday Park

Terry and Billy O'Neill with Dr Tom Stark and Victor Leonard (Milk Cup Chairman)

Plans for holiday chalets on 20 acres of the Mill Road site in Portstewart were rejected too even though Billy insisted that the land had been zoned for recreation and a tourist centre which he argued effectively meant that the planners were turning down their own plans.

Billy appealed and put in an application for 'development' and a public inquiry took place at Coleraine Town Hall where the O'Neills' QC challenged the planners' objections to caravans at Mill Road. He insisted that the application was indeed for 'development' and that the word 'caravans' hadn't been used.

"When we came out the barrister said we won the battle but we weren't sure if he had won the war," reflects Billy who in the end got planning permission for houses on the 20 acres site and for a tourist development on the other seven acres for caravans and camping.

Work on developing the Mill Road Holiday Village, as it was known, started in 1979.

He says: "The planners wanted us to create the park in what we believed was the wrong way round with camping and touring caravans on a very steep hill and static homes on level ground. The issue was that static owners usually only change their homes every 15 years whereas touring caravans and camping could be changed nightly. That involved having to reverse a touring caravan on a hill which could be dangerous for young people and senior citizens

"Gradually we got a change of heart with static on the hill. At what is now the Millfield Holiday Park at Mill Road there are 70 static holiday homes along with 12 houses and 12 apartments.

"In 1981, I acquired the town's old reservoir which was a danger to the children on the park. I thought about using the old reservoir to build a new family home but I was advised against it."

The following year Billy was approached by footballing legend Bertie Peacock, the former Northern Ireland international who had played for Celtic and Coleraine. Bertie and a number of other football men who were planning Northern Ireland's first Milk Cup tournament for youth teams from all over the world needed accommodation for the visiting players and their support staff. Billy offered them 34 units which could sleep up to five young people and the organisers gladly accepted.

In another move which benefitted young people Billy lent land to the police in Portstewart and Castlerock where youngsters from both sides of the community were able to camp again free of charge.

In the early 80s Billy sold land to developers in the Triangle area but his own hopes of building a hotel at Ballyreagh using some of his substantial profits were dashed after he was refused a Northern Ireland Tourist Board grant at a time when he says a number of other projects put forward by other entrepreneurs obtained financial support.

Deflated but not defeated Billy pushed ahead with the development of O'Neill's Causeway Coast apartments at Ballyreagh and got planning permission for 20 three-bedroom apartments for holiday rentals (the first of its kind on the North Coast) and on April 12, 1985 they were officially opened by the Department of Economic Development's Sir David Fell whose department had provided grant aid. The same year saw a massive fillip for Billy when he and his team were honoured with a British Airways Tourism Endeavour award for the new complex.

The local papers covered the prestigious award which the Coleraine Chronicle said was for the O'Neills Causeway Coast Apartments on the Ballyreagh Road between Portrush and Portstewart.

The coveted award was handed over by Eurovision song contest winner Dana at a gala night in Belfast and a recording of the proceedings were later screened by Ulster Television.

The citation said the award was designed to acknowledge and encourage special efforts made by individuals and groups in tourism endeavour and the presenting of Northern Ireland's more positive image abroad.

The Chronicle article also included a report on a visit by an influential American businessman Bill Ward to the holiday complex at Ballyreagh and on how impressed he had been with what he saw in the O'Neills' development which was preparing to open a new grill room and restaurant for the forthcoming holiday season in 1986.

Some years later there was another bonus for the O'Neills in the shape of an unexpected invitation to attend a garden party with the Queen at Buckingham Palace.

Billy and Lily told local newspapers that they at first thought the letter from London was a hoax because they couldn't think what they had done to deserve the invitation though they later decided it may have been in recognition for their efforts for the tourism industry in their area.

"Whatever the reason it certainly was a tremendous honour for us," Billy told the press adding that his only regret was that he didn't have the chance to speak to the Queen or the Duke of Edinburgh.

Looking back now to his tourism endeavours Billy says in the early 80s he was disappointed that Northern Ireland's tourism chiefs didn't give him the sort of support they were giving inward investors particularly for a hotel that he was planning at Ballyreagh.

In 1985 he had received planning approval for the aforementioned O'Neill's restaurant and grill room at Ballyreagh but he was initially refused a grant though a year later he was able to go ahead with the hotel which was then used by Milk Cup officials and for darts, pool, snooker and bridge tournaments.

The newspapers had been full of stories about business and tourism people crying out for more hotels on the north coast at a time when some existing establishments were being knocked down to make way for the construction of more and more holiday apartments for families looking for second homes in Portrush and Portstewart.

Billy was convinced his hotel would be a roaring success and his planning for it was typically meticulous with the O'Neills travelling far and wide to acquire the right fixtures

Dana presenting Lily and Billy with British Airways Tourism Endeavour Award 1985

Official Opening of apartments 1986 by Sir David Fell

Causeway Coast Hotel, Apartments and Conference Centre

Joe Loss Orchestra

Conference Room Set for Lion's International Dinner Dance

A few of the Staff

Conference Room

Entertainment six nights a week

and fittings for their new venture. But they also got a pleasant surprise they hadn't been bargaining on at a furniture show in the Burlington Hotel at Ballsbridge in Dublin.

As they walked down a corridor in the Burlington where they had been staying Billy spied a familiar face of one of his all-time dancing heroes.

Billy was convinced the distinguished looking man was none other than the dancer and movie star Fred Astaire who was a frequent visitor to Ireland but Lily was sceptical. So Billy hurried back in the man's direction to try to confirm his suspicions.

"It was indeed Fred Astaire and I just had to tell him how much Lily and I admired his work and how much he had inspired us and our dancing. I then asked if his partner Ginger Rogers happened to be with him but sadly she wasn't. It was rumoured that Fred was in Ireland to make a movie but to this day I don't know what it was. I thought it might have been The Field which was filmed in Leenane, County Galway but I know now that he wasn't in that one." says Billy. "I must have seen every film he was in. "

Before long O'Neill's Causeway Coast Hotel had 21 bedrooms and a conference room which was used extensively by government departments, schools and organisations like the Rotary Club and the Lions Club plus there was a wine bar.

A glossy, full-colour brochure extolled the virtues of the hotel. Complete with pictures it said: "A warm welcome awaits you at The Causeway Coast Hotel where quality, service and hospitality are a way of life. Whatever your requirements we have the accommodation, facilities and services to suit you. Business visitor, conference delegate, sporting break or family holiday our friendly staff are dedicated to ensuring your complete enjoyment and satisfaction."

The profile of the hotel soared with the introduction of entertainment nights which during the summer months drew massive crowds to see comedian Gene Fitzpatrick on Tuesday nights; cabaret group Clubsound on Wednesday nights and stars like May McFettridge or the fast emerging comic Patrick Kielty on Thursday nights.

Dinner dances pulled in the crowds to the O'Neill Suite on Saturday nights and a Sunday carvery ensured that the hotel was busy then too.

What the brochure called 'the old world charm' of the Dunluce Room was popular for weddings and for appearances by local music acts like the talented duo, Plug and Dominic.

The booklet also promised 'fun' in the Tramways Steak Bar and 'great Craic' in the La Bon Wine Bar. It added that there were also 'pleasant lounges and a snooker room which provided for relaxation.'

Also included in the brochure was a short guide to the attractions near the hotel on the north coast plus potted histories of the Giant's Causeway and Dunluce Castle.

Memorably for Billy, one of the UK's finest musical ensembles, the Joe Loss Orchestra also played at the hotel. Joe Loss had died in 1990 but his band continued to play under his name, much in the same way that the Glenn Miller Orchestra who went on performing

Lily, Billy and employee Maureen McCaughen

National Snooker Competition

Tram Room Restaurant

Royal Canadian Mounted Police and guests

Mayor, William King opening O'Neill's Restaurant

RUC dinner

Sir John Swinson and Lady Swinson

Coleraine Mayor's Show winners

Guests at opening of restaurant

David, Florence and Lily with Pat Jennings

Sir Alex Ferguson and Billy O'Neill

Speedy Moore with Lions Club guest from USA

after the American maestro's disappearance on a flight from England to France during WW2.

Billy's booking of the Joe Loss Orchestra for their only concert in Ireland grabbed the attention of newspapers here. Indeed the legendary journalist Eddie McIlwaine ran a piece in the Belfast Telegraph which revealed that Joe Loss, in person, had brought his band to Portstewart in the 1950s to open the Top Hat Ballroom under the name of the Strand Ballroom.

Country and western music was also popular at the Causeway Coast Hotel with entire weekends devoted to entertainers like the versatile Crawford Bell who frequently played on records with Belfast rock singer Van Morrison.

In September 1994 the Causeway Coast Hotel came under the wing of the Best Western Hotels group. Billy says: "They only market hotels, you know, they don't own them.

Jerry McCauly NITB opening Millfield Holiday Park 1982

Individual hotel owners like me joined them because they were the biggest hotel marketing company in the world. I paid them to strengthen my advertising and so on."

Mayor John White, Christmas Window Competition sponsors

Billy receiving Melvin Jones Fellow Lions International Award

Sponsoring Milk Cup

Football presentation

Event at Ballyreagh, Causeway Coast Hotel

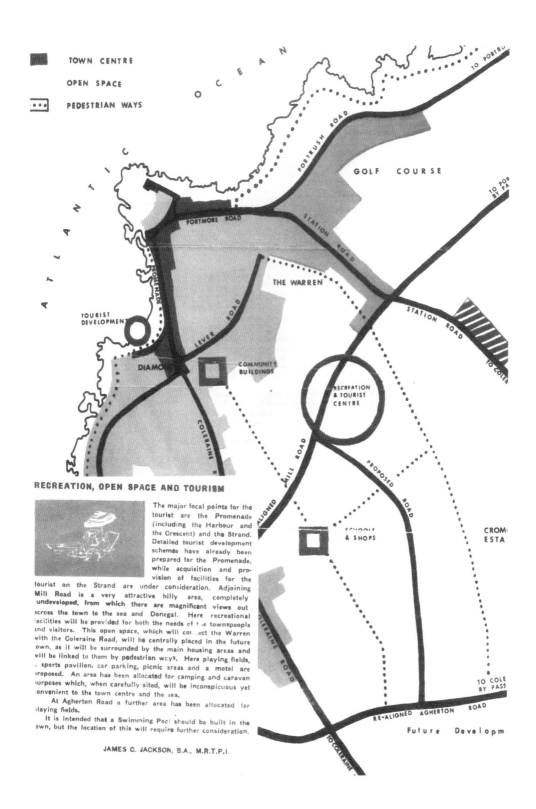

TOWN CENTRE

OPEN SPACE

PEDESTRIAN WAYS

O C E A N

A T L A N T I C

GOLF COURSE

TO PORTRU

TO POR
BY PA

PORTRUSH ROAD

STATION ROAD

FORTMORE ROAD

THE WARREN

STATION ROAD

TO COTER

PROMENADE

TOURIST
DEVELOPMENT

LEVER ROAD

DIAMOND

COMMUNITY
BUILDINGS

RECREATION
& TOURIST
CENTRE

COLERAINE R

MILL ROAD

PROPOSED ROAD

SCHOOLS
& SHOPS

CROM
ESTA

COLERAINE ROAD

RE-ALIGNED

TO COLE
BY PASS

RE-ALIGNED AGHERTON ROAD

Future Developm

TO COLERAINE

RECREATION, OPEN SPACE AND TOURISM

The major focal points for the tourist are the Promenade (including the Harbour and the Crescent) and the Strand. Detailed tourist development schemes have already been prepared for the Promenade, while acquisition and provision of facilities for the tourist on the Strand are under consideration. Adjoining Mill Road is a very attractive hilly area, completely undeveloped, from which there are magnificent views out across the town to the sea and Donegal. Here recreational facilities will be provided for both the needs of the townspeople and visitors. This open space, which will connect the Warren with the Coleraine Road, will be centrally placed in the future town, as it will be surrounded by the main housing areas and will be linked to them by pedestrian ways. Here playing fields, sports pavilion, car parking, picnic areas and a motel are proposed. An area has been allocated for camping and caravan purposes which, when carefully sited, will be inconspicuous yet convenient to the town centre and the sea.

At Agherton Road a further area has been allocated for playing fields.

It is intended that a Swimming Pool should be built in the town, but the location of this will require further consideration.

JAMES C. JACKSON, B.A., M.R.T.P.I.

98

14

A nightmare ending to the Causeway Coast dream

B illy O'Neill had more dreams for his hotel. He wanted a bigger and even better venue. And he aimed high with a proposal to extend the hotel with another 80 bedrooms and an exhibition centre. Which he says sporting bodies, the media and politicians all agreed was a must for the north coast to accommodate the increasing number of tourists especially visitors on coach tours. Billy went public with his concerns that the north coast didn't have enough bedrooms. He told a meeting of

Billy in his office

the Causeway Coast Tourist Development Association that he was constantly having to turn away guests because he was fully booked.

He also said that Portrush and Portstewart were losing out to towns like Ballymena and Limavady because they simply didn't have enough beds for visitors.

As support for Billy's extension plans grew he says wasn't encouraged by the response, or lack of it, from officials in charge of statutory tourism bodies, who he didn't believe shared his enthusiasm for providing more beds on the north coast.. But Billy and his people still came up with plans and costings for turning their visions into reality. In 1994 a series of letters supporting the O'Neill project were sent to the Northern Ireland Tourist Board (NITB) and even to Downing Street to the Prime Minister of the time John Major.

One of Northern Ireland's most respected business commentators John Simpson entered the fray in 1994 calling for answers and clarity from the NITB on their policy towards the expansion of the hotel sector.

Simpson wrote that decisions on grant aid for hotel developments had given little clear evidence of a coherent plan for future expansions. He said: "Many hotel owners believe that the Tourist Board is unfair to existing hotel businesses. There is a suspicion that financial assistance tends to go to inward investments in preference to local projects. Certainly the economics of a hotel, using borrowed funds, can be badly shaken by a deal, agreed in private with the Tourist Board, to grant aid another hotel in the same area. The local owner has no right to be consulted and may not even know of the project until it is announced, even though the business might be damaged."

On August 7 1994 the Sunday Life newspaper in Belfast ran a story about Billy's plans for the Causeway Coast Hotel, saying 'crunch time' was fast approaching for his multi-million pound development to boost tourism in Portrush. The article said: "Hopes for providing the resort with a new flagship hotel hang in the balance as tourist board chiefs consider how much funding they will provide. Billy O'Neill, owner of the Causeway Coast Hotel, has drawn up ambitious plans for the scheme, based on the outcome of report drawn up by the Northern Ireland Tourist Board and Coleraine Council to identify tourism needs in the area. Mr O'Neill hopes to extend his hotel to provide a major exhibition and conference centre. leisure centre and additional bedrooms at a cost of £4.25 million. The scheme would create 117 new jobs and provide Portrush with a hotel capable of hosting major sporting and heritage events. Mr O'Neill, who has built up his business over a number of years, is prepared to invest £2m of his own money in the scheme, and hopes to secure grant aid of 50pc. "I have come up with a plan which is tailor-made for the area and I believe it should be encouraged," he said.

Portrush Chamber of Commerce backed the idea and Billy continued to push for grants to be awarded to local businesses as well as to inward investors, claiming the disparity in funding needed to be addressed.

Billy took his case to a meeting on May 13, 1995 with the then Minister for Tourism in Northern Ireland Baroness Denton of Wakefield and almost a year later he was still fighting his fight for more help.

Later still Coleraine Borough Council sent a letter to Baroness Denton on March 3, 1997 saying their Economic Development Committee had just heard a presentation from Billy O'Neill outlining his proposals for further development of the Causeway Coast Hotel to provide more bedrooms, leisure facilities and an exhibition centre.

The council's Deputy Chief Executive Mr H.W.T Moore wrote: "Such a proposal was enthusiastically supported by Council given the frequently identified need for more high quality accommodation in the area. However Council was advised by Mr O'Neill that the project would not be viable on the basis of the current level of capital grant being offered by the Northern Ireland Tourist Board which was claimed to be well below that offered to other similar projects in the area. Council would be most anxious to see this project proceed and would welcome your personal intervention to break what appears to be an impasse in negotiations between Mr O'Neill and Tourist Board officials; even a marginally improved offer may be sufficient to break the log-jam."

Billy sent a letter to the investment director of the NITB saying that with a grant from them and his own investments a 'lovely' 101 bedroom holiday complex with apartments, conference and leisure facilities plus an exhibition centre and railway halt could have been provided to meet the needs of Portrush at a cost of £6.6million.

"I negotiated for seven years with the Department of Economic Development and the NITB but to no avail," says Billy who claims he was encouraged by some officials to sell one of his caravan parks to 'build my bedrooms' but he refused after querying whether or not the people behind other tourist ventures in Northern Ireland had sold any of their businesses to fund their projects. (Billy says he also rejected any suggestions that the statutory organisations should have preference shares in the extended hotel if grants were awarded to him. His reasoning he says was that he had built up his business entirely on his own and didn't want to have to work alongside or under any new partners.)

Billy ruefully accepted that a grant for 80 more bedrooms and an exhibition hall was '99 per cent nil' and knowing that he had nothing to lose sought the help of the Rev Ian Paisley MP in asking parliamentary questions at Westminster on a number of occasions.

Billy still has a bulging ring-binder of all the letters that were exchanged between him, local politicians and the authorities, especially the NITB and government departments like the Department of Economic Development. The folder runs into hundreds of thousands of

West Strand Portrush

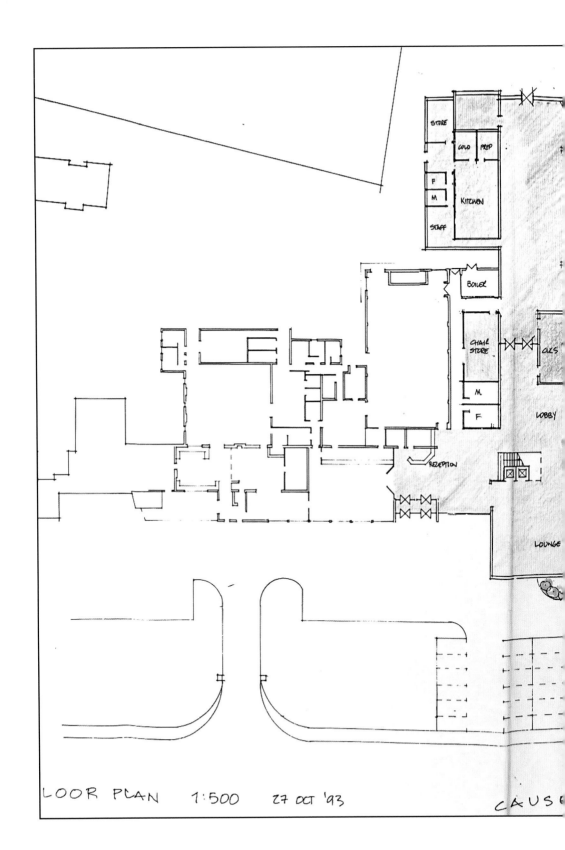

STORE

COLD PREP

F

M

KITCHEN

STAFF

BOILER

CHAIR STORE

M

F

LOBBY

RECEPTION

LOUNGE

FLOOR PLAN   1:500   27 OCT '93

CAUSE

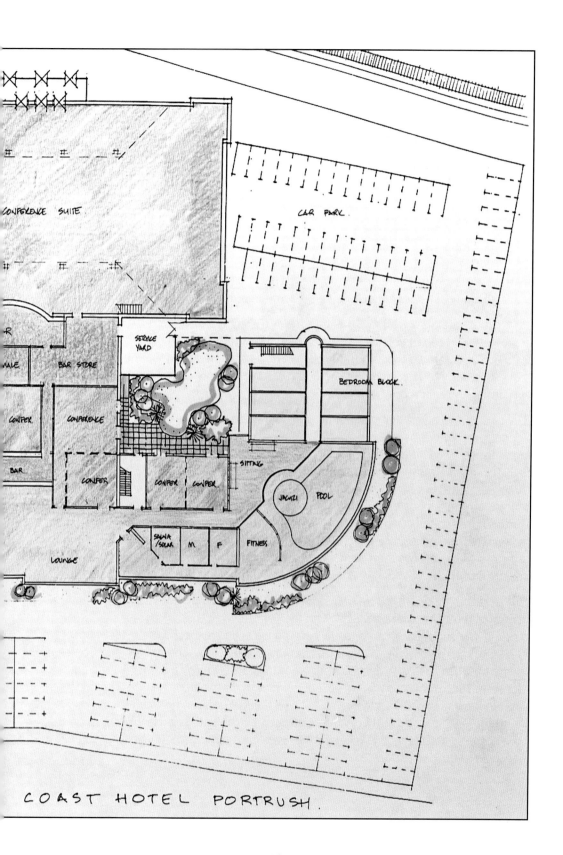

CONFERENCE SUITE

CAR PARK

SERVICE YARD

ALE   BAR STORE

BEDROOM BLOCK

R

CONFEX.   CONFERENCE

SITTING

BAR.   CONFER   CONFER CONFER

JACUZI   POOL

SAUNA /SOLAR   M   F   FITNESS

LOUNGE

COAST HOTEL PORTRUSH.

words in the letters and also includes some of Billy's 'frustrated' observations about the way the tourism industry was being run in Northern Ireland. One of his notes said that local hoteliers who had put up with 25 years of the troubles and bombs and bullets had been rewarded 'not with a clap on the back but rather a kick in the teeth.'

Billy also researched funding which had been allotted to a number of new hotel businesses and restaurants and claimed there was an imbalance between the money that was going to inward investors and the aid that was being granted to local entrepreneurs. Billy knew that his assertions did not make him a popular figure among some in the hospitality industry Bodies and he claimed he was being bullied in some quarters something 'which I will not accept.'

Billy was furious with 'spurious' suggestions that were put forward that the Causeway Coast Hotel had been the subject of customer complaints to the Tourist Board. He says that one issue that was followed up by the NITB was about a hotel guest who was unhappy that a cheque he had tendered for a £2.50 hamburger had been declined.

"When the hotel manager saw the letter from the complainant he remembered that the customer had been unable to provide any identification to back up his cheque. The man from the NITB tore up the letter," says Billy who was also amazed that he was told how a request for a three star rating for the hotel was turned down because there were no net curtains on the bedroom windows.

Billy says he explained that most of his guests wanted an uninterrupted sea view but that net curtains were provided on windows of rooms that had a less attractive outlook. On legal advice Billy photographed every hotel on the north coast and as far away as Ballymena and Antrim to provide proof that none of them had net curtains. He won his three star rating. But he still wasn't satisfied at what he believed was the unfair treatment of local business people who throughout the years of the troubles had striven to keep Northern Ireland going and to give the NITB a product to sell. He provided a dossier of figures showing what he argued was the unjustifiable preferential treatment to inward investors whose profits from tourist endeavours like hotels were ploughed back into the countries of origin.

Billy sold the hotel in 1998 and he says: "Most of the family hotels are gone now. And instead of receiving a pat on the back for their efforts from tourism bosses the owners got a kick on the bum. Many of the family hotels have been knocked down by developers who built apartments for sale. "O'Neill's Causeway Coast Hotel, Apartments and Conference Centre were demolished within a few years and instead of gaining a further 80 bedrooms and tourist facilities, 21 bedrooms were lost along with the 60 bedrooms in the apartments that were knocked down." Billy however was still on the look-out for more caravan parks. But his interest in one in Portrush that had been owned by the late Sam Henry cooled. So many developers wanted the land to meet the new growing trend for apartments in the area that 'I was well and truly outbid.'

15

Stranocum Hall; objectionable objections and a mother's wisdom

B illy and Lily's thoughts now turned to finding a new home for themselves but they could never have envisaged what they would buy at the end of their search. For on their return from a viewing of a house in the village of Dervock, fate took them in a totally different direction. En route to call with Billy's brother David the O'Neill's spotted a 'for sale' sign on a house on the Fivey Road in Stranocum. But it wasn't just any old house. It was Stranocum Hall an imposing Georgian mansion which was just four miles from the O'Neills' home though Billy didn't even know it existed until that chance drive-past.

Stranocum Hall winter 1999

With Billy's mother having been born even nearer to Stranocum he felt he was going back to his roots when he and Lily travelled to see the Hall that hadn't been lived in for 40 years but had been partially renovated by local builder John Stewart and his two sons.

An estate agent's listing for the house in 1996 had included an assessment from the Ulster Architectural Heritage Society highlighting the importance of the residence which it said was once 'one of the finest gentleman's residences in the area.'

The estate agent said that while the Hall had been uninhabited for many years the house and gardens remained worthy of investment and rescue.

Says Billy who had once considered purchasing Cromore House in Portstewart: "Lily and I liked Stranocum Hall and decided that we would go for it if we got it at the right price. I told John Stewart that my father was a Ballymena man and that people from his town never paid the asking price."

"Eventually we agreed on a deal that suited us both. And the first thing we did was to bring a full amenity double glazed 38ft Pemberton caravan with under floor insulation and central heating onto the Stranocum site. I was 59 and couldn't wait to put the overalls back on to do a bit of manual work again. I joked with our friends that our two sons had put us out to Stranocum to graze but it was far from the truth.

"After settling into the caravan, Tony O'Brien who was a carpenter we we enjoyed working with for years at the hotel and caravan parks was brought in to help with Stranocum Hall. He thought he was going to be there for a couple of months but we employed him at Stranocum for over a year with other tradesmen.

"It was the first time the house had had electricity, water and sewage in it."

Stranocum prior to restoration

As well as rolling up his sleeves at Stranocum Billy rolled back the years to research the history of the Hall and uncovered a remarkable heritage in the house which was originally built around 1755 by a family from Scotland called Hutchinson. George Hutchinson had arrived to settle in Stranocum in 1598 and one of his descendants Archibald Hutchinson was an MP for Hastings.

Another George Hutchinson was a more controversial character who had the nickname 'Bloody' and not without good reason. He was born at Stranocum and went on to become a magistrate in Ballymoney where he cultivated a reputation as a ruthless judge. In 1798, at the age of 37, he was given the responsibility of putting down a rebellion by the United Irishmen movement and punishing the leaders in whatever way he deemed fit, including by hanging.

One United Irishman, Samuel Dunlop was hanged from a tree by the roadside at the rather inappropriately named Pleasure Step near the townland of Bendooragh in 1799.

Other leaders who were executed included Alexander Gamble, William Caulfield, William Adams and Samuel Bonniton and it's said that to make an example of them Hutchinson ordered that several of them should be hanged from the Clock Tower at the top of Ballymoney's Main Street.

Later on the rebels exacted their revenge. Local United Irishmen looted the Hall which was empty apart from servants, taking not only guns but also food and spirits from the kitchen cellars.

Another 'spirit' was said to haunt Stranocum Hall - that of 'Bloody' Hutchinson who lived to the ripe old age of 103.

One story from the archives said that Hutchinson's spirit is actually seen every Friday the 13th and on Halloween as he limps his way along Main Street with a large metal ball chained to his ankle before stopping and turning back again to his final resting place in the burial ground in the site of the old parish church which holds over 400 gravestones, the oldest dating from 1610.

The legend is that Hutchinson's spirit will disappear forever if he can be prevented from completing his journey to the graveyard beside Ballymoney's famous Old Church Tower. Others say that if anyone is lucky enough to see him even from afar they will disappear for ever.

Local people say one man was so drunk that he accepted a challenge to spend the night in the churchyard where Hutchinson is buried and after sobering up the next morning he was naked with his hair having turned white and he was speaking in gibberish about having seen ghosts.

Billy O'Neill was later to hear stories of Hutchinson's ghost again and again along with a claim that a 'grey lady' also haunted Stranocum Hall though no-one ever saw any of the spectres.

Ironically while Hutchinson's fearsome reputation was well-known he is also remembered by many people as a patron of the community around Stranocum where it's said he collected money and donated land to help the building of Catholic churches in Dunloy and Ballymoney.

Archibald Hutchinson Esq.

Silhouette of George (Bloody) Hutchinson and family

Aerial photo of Stranocum Hall

The history books record that after Stranocum Hall was pillaged another member of the Hutchinson family – Lieutenant Dick Hutchinson of the Dunluce Cavalry - shot and wounded a local man called Neil McGarry after he made a joke about the looting.

Another man Richard Caldwell was convicted of treason after testimony from a Stranocum servant, James Crosbie. Caldwell was ordered to be hung in Ballymoney and his head severed from his body to be placed on a pike outside the Market House in the town. But his wealthy father used his influence and his son was pardoned on condition that he went to America and never returned. His father also agreed to pay the King £1,000 in two lots of £500.

Many many years later Stranocum Hall featured in a very different narrative linked to the Ulster Volunteer Force's resistance to Irish Home Rule.

The Protestant volunteers had organised for arms shipments to be ferried into ports like Larne in 1914 and one of the most famous ships was the Clyde Valley whose guns were soon being secreted in stockpiles across Ulster including at Stranocum Hall.

One account relating to the operation in County Antrim said that a man called Stewart Moore and his men 'spent a disappointingly dull night guarding Stranocum village.'

It went on: "They were to prevent police from entering the village, but there was no sight of the Royal Irish Constabulary through the night. At 4.30am tired and sleepy, they were ordered home. The next afternoon, Stewart Moore drove to Stranocum House and found his Uncle James with a revolver in hand, organising a group of men who were loading a car with bundles of rifles, wrapped in canvas. They had originally been delivered at 7 a.m. but a disturbing report had come through that there were five policemen fishing on the river nearby with only one rod between them. It was decided that the rifles had better be distributed around the country for safe-keeping.Stewart Moore put a bundle of guns under a rug on the floor of his cart, stopped briefly at a neighbour's for afternoon tea, then returned home, where with stifled excitement, he and his sister hid the rifles after nightfall in an unused loft above the scullery. Shortly afterwards the guns would be handed out to his Volunteers for the first time."

The fascinating history of Stranocum Hall is the subject of many other books in the shops and essays on the internet. And it has also featured in a wide range of talks for local history societies who've included the Hall on bus tours.

A Northern Ireland wartime website also explains why a plaque was erected at Stranocum Hall in 2005 to mark a well-publicised event during WW2 when the building and the outhouses were converted to accommodate child evacuees who had been re-located from Malta. But on November 20, 1944 there was a near tragedy.

A Vickers Wellington JA308 bomber on a night navigation exercise to Rathlin Island from Empire Air Navigation School at RAF Shawbury in Shropshire in England developed engine trouble and when the pilot attempted a forced landing by moonlight the aircraft lost altitude over an orchard at Stranocum Hall. Several tree tops were sheared off and the plane crashed at the corner of the walled orchard.

Wellington bomber

The Wellington Mark VIII caught fire but the five crew members survived, thanks to the bravery of staff at the Hall who helped pull the airmen from the wreckage. The staff later received a letter from the RAF thanking them for their courageous actions. There was also praise for the plane's crew who had managed to avoid hitting Stranocum Hall and saving the lives of the people inside.

An investigation showed that in the poor weather and icy conditions the bomber had lost the use of both its altimeter and airspeed indicator.

The plaque says: "The crash site of the RAF Wellington bomber which came down at Stranocum House on November 20 1944. Fortunately the five crew members survived due to the courageous action of local people." Quite bizarrely there was an odd footnote to the crash after a young man was charged with stealing an indicator light from the Wellington which he had found 100 yards from the plane. A magistrate fined him £1 and it was revealed that other souvenir hunters had taken other items from the scene but they were never seen again.

Newspaper reports from the time said that as well as the young Maltese children who were housed at Stranocum, elderly residents from Gibraltar were also living there.

The account added: "By April 1945, the ageing residents were becoming impatient to return home; not even repeat visits by the Stranocum Dance Band seemed to appease them. It would be several months before they could be repatriated and Stranocum House returned to the Ford-Hutchinson family." But while Billy was garnering more information about the history of the Stranocum he and Lily were also busying themselves with their endeavours to turn the house into their dream home. Billy bought pine from an antiques shop in Coleraine to put down on top of the original flooring to strengthen it and a new set of stairs was added up to the first floor. John Stewart hadn't installed bathrooms or toilets because he knew from experience that new owners of old houses usually preferred to bring their own touches. And that's something that Billy and Lily revelled in. Says Billy: "I must have been to a hundred auctions and dozens of antique shops searching for furniture and other items. Mealy's auctions in Castlecomer in County Kilkenny was a great source for the larger pieces of furniture. The choosing of the wallpaper and paint was done nearer home at the firm of George Patton Paints and Wallpapers and we were in Stranocum Hall for Christmas 1998 though it wasn't fully furnished. But that didn't deter us from having a family party on Boxing Day when we invited around 65 family members and friends in on what was a stormy night, a night that proved to be eventful after the lights suddenly went out and the winds blew down three trees, one across the laneway to the house. The cellars had been used for a drinks reception and Lily had prepared all the food by gas. We were lucky in that we had loads of candles about the place and they added to the atmosphere of our party where the mulled wine flowed along with the stories, some of which were sad when missing members of the family like my brother Eddie were remembered by the guests who included 20 of his relatives. The O'Neills bought the gate lodge at Stranocum in January 1999 and a few months later they had an addition to their family with the arrival of their grandson, Ryan O'Neill. Billy bade farewell to an old friend soon afterwards as he watched the demolition of the Causeway Coast Hotel for development though he was able to buy a number of fixtures like tables and chairs for Stranocum Hall which was soon pressed into service to host a social event for Ballymoney Rotary Club. Billy cleared out the Bell Tower barn across the way from Stranocum Hall for a barbecue and a dance floor from the old Coleraine Borough Council offices at Cloonavin was purchased at auction.The Hall's farmer neighbour, James McConaghie came calling and in next or no time Billy bought an acre of land from him which he intended to use for car parking on the night of the barbecue.

Billy also utilised a power hose from a caravan park to remove white lime covering attractive stonework on Stranocum's coach shed and his protective equipment was so all encompassing that his little grandchildren Arlene and David who were Stephen's children didn't recognise him because he wasn't wearing his traditional garb – a suit.

Arlene was later to respond to seeing Billy and his two brothers Hughie and David together in the same room by saying she was seeing three grandads all at the same time.

With Stranocum Hall becoming more and more like a home Billy turned his attentions to buying new property in his hometown of Ballymoney.

The speculation in the area was that the one and a quarter acre site would sell for over a million pounds but Billy got it for half the price.

Included in the sale in Linen Hall Street in Ballymoney was the Kosey Korner pub which allowed Billy to transfer the alcohol licence for 14 nights in any one year to Stranocum. "So that was Stranocum Hall totally set up for fund raising events for charity," says Billy who had plans drawn up for an entertainment complex including four cinema screens, a bingo hall, a night club, a restaurant plus community facilities or a museum. Billy met motorcycling ace Joey Dunlop in his bar in Ballymoney to discuss opening that museum in his name but he died in a tragic accident during a race in Estonia in 2000, the scene of which Billy and Lily were later to visit on one of their foreign holidays.

Meetings were also held with experienced professionals in the cinema, sporting and night club worlds about running the new complex.

The very mention of a cinema in the plans sparked a frenzy of interest in Ballymoney where there'd been no picture house for years. Indeed a survey had revealed that 85 per cent of people in Ballymoney attended the cinema on a regular basis with 79 per cent going to Coleraine to see the latest movies with five per cent heading to Portrush and one per cent travelling to Ballymena for their cinematic outings.

So excited did local people become that there was even fanciful talk in the newspapers that Ballymena-born Hollywood superstar actor Liam Neeson might even be persuaded to perform an official opening ceremony.

The plans and designs for the transformation of Ballymoney's town centre appeared in the local newspapers which warmly welcomed the proposals that they wrote about in great detail as the weeks and months went on.

The Ballymoney Times said the local council had thrown their weight behind calls to secure financial backing from the International Fund for Ireland for the proposals which also included a hotel.

The paper also reported that the Department of Environment had responded positively to the plan. quoting architect Jim Donnelly as saying: "The plan strikes a good balance between modern and traditional design. The majority of the development will be three stories with four stories at the corners. We feel the scheme brings life and vitality back into the centre of Ballymoney especially after 6pm."

But the plans were thrown into disarray after a shop owner in Ballymoney refused to sell it to Billy who soon afterwards added a new caravan park to his portfolio though the purchase of the Edgewater Holiday Park at Minerstown close to Tyrella beach in County Down which was a long way from his existing sites.

Billy's nephew Loren – his brother Hughie's son – now owns and manages Edgewater.

Back in Portstewart Billy drew up plans for a residential development on the Burnside caravan park which would incorporate 95 houses and apartments

In 2000 under the banner of Bonalston Caravans Ltd, Billy's son Terry bought the Ballyleese Town and Country caravan Park in Portstewart from Peter Young and a couple of years later 70 acres of what was known as hope land to try and enhance the Ballyleese Park.

Billy planned to roll the profits from the Burnside re-development into his project in Ballymoney but his plans for the caravan park met with objections from a number of residents in Portstewart in a campaign which was led by some prominent figures in the local area.

The scale of the campaign shocked Billy who says he believed that it wasn't everything that it seemed and that some supposed 'objectors' assured him that they hadn't actually signed their names to letters to the planning authorities.

The row over the new development was reported on a regular basis in the local newspapers and debate over the planning application swung back and forward generating a lot of controversy in the Triangle area.

Billy says he has copies of all 384 letters of objection to Burnside and he questions whether or not they were all actually sent by the people whose names appeared in the correspondence. One man, he says, told him that he'd received an acknowledgement from the planning authorities of a letter that he had never sent. Billy suspected that some personal animosities towards him came into play during the campaign. It reminded him, he says, of objections to him getting an entertainment licence for his hotel at Ballyreagh some years earlier.

Just as he was upset about a perceived lack of support from tourism organisations, Billy was questioning why he was encountering so many hurdles as he tried to press forward with new plans for developments particularly in Portstewart.

The debate that raged on the north coast was whether or not any more people who wanted second homes in the holiday hotspots were entitled to fulfil their wishes or if some people who were resident in the area simply didn't want anyone else to settle and enjoy living in Portstewart.

The changing nature of caravan sites in urban settings meant that it was difficult to improve and extend according to Billy O'Neill who says the old caravan parks in town struggle to accommodate the size of modern holiday caravans that have to be at least 5M apart where as apartments need only be 12 inches apart.

"All I ever wanted was a level playing field to create a family business and in the process to enhance tourism" says Billy. "In the end it took eight years to obtain planning for Burnside - about the same sort of time that Britain took to fight two World Wars!!.

My message to some of the politicians and planners back in the day was that I felt they were actually hampering progress when their job was to facilitate the improvement of infrastructure and prosperity, not to hinder it. "

Billy says he still feels aggrieved that he had to face so many difficulties in his drive to push ahead with his tourism projects. And he has a huge number of files containing scores of letters between him and the planning and tourism authorities to remind him, if he should ever need it, of the hurdles that were placed in his way.

"I like to think that I always acted with integrity. I always remembered what my mother said when I left Ballymoney - that while education is nice to have, good manners and honesty will take you as far and you do not have to go to University to learn that," he insists.

16

The Lord and Lady of the Manor at 'Downton Abbey'

The difficulties over planning and support from the tourist authorities didn't deter Billy and Lily from driving forward with their ambitious renovations to Stranocum Hall where their first barbecue on behalf of Ballymoney's Rotary Club had been a roaring success As they set about their refurbishments the O'Neills went to great lengths to hire the finest tradesmen and bought the best fittings and lighting available, including the highest class chandeliers that they could purchase and they also sought out antique fireplaces for the Hall.

Billy and Lily with guests

Billy's favourite part of the house was the kitchen and wine cellar for which he acquired new stone floors and recreated staff bedrooms were installed in the cellar too.

Hilariously however Billy tells the story of how went to an auction in nearby Dunloy to buy an old range for the kitchen and came home with a Massey Ferguson tractor, the first purchase for what become Billy's agriculture collection.

Most of the contents of the Coachman's Inn at Dunmurry which was closing were bought at auction and an 18ft black oak bar with background mirrors and shelves made a striking centrepiece for the Stranocum barn.

A stone fountain that had been at the front of the Coachman's was re-assembled in full working order outside Billy and Lily's home and goldfish were also added to it.

Other extras were security gates with huge lions on top plus a new double garage and a conservatory which was where Billy and Lily liked to live when it wasn't too hot or cold.

Billy and Stephen went to so many auctions that Lily nicknamed them Steptoe and Son and if her husband went on his own she called him Lovejoy!

One of Billy's most treasured purchases at an auction was a rare original 6ft high poster made of silk promoting the John Wayne/Maureen O'Hara movie 'The Quiet Man' filmed in and around the Galway village of Cong. Billy was filmed clinching the deal at Wilson's Auctions in Mallusk and when he appeared on a TV news bulletin his son Terry happened to see him while he was on a Coleraine Round Table trip to Dublin.

The O'Neill family got another laugh the next morning when an auctioneer rang to ask if he would sell the poster to broadcaster Eamonn Holmes who's a big John Wayne fan. Billy didn't like to disappoint Eamonn but the answer was a firm 'no.' Billy and Lily were soon throwing themselves enthusiastically into the life of Stranocum and at a community association meeting they came up with the idea of racing plastic ducks on the River Bush which ran through the village.

Stranocum Hall hosted a barbecue during the festival week and Billy opened up more space in the hayloft. The event was again an unqualified success with upwards of 700 tickets sold.

Back at the main house the improvements went on apace and the highlight was a large dining room table and chairs that could sit 14 people. Four poster beds were bought for two bedrooms including the one where Billy and Lily slept.

But Billy was no dozer when it came to indulging his hobbies like collecting cast-iron tractor seats and he became a member of the Cast Iron Seat Society. One of his first buys was a seat branded Weir because that was his middle name and then came a Jones because that was the maiden name of Lily's granny. Billy got a tip-off that another collector in Stranraer might be willing to sell his assortment of seats that numbered up to 50.

Billy and Lily called with John Bell on their way home from a continental trip and bought most of his collection which he had wanted to make sure weren't split up.

At the last count Billy had amassed no fewer than 264 seats, a collection which was second only to one in Larne apparently.

Later when the O'Neills moved back to Portstewart Billy put up all but two of the seats – the Weir and the Jones – up for auction in England. The two that were kept are in a small museum that he now has in Portstewart.

In Stranocum the festive week duck race was a massive hit with huge crowds coming to enjoy the spectacle that was to be repeated on an annual basis.

The barbecue was also adjudged to be a winner by scores of guests who dined on chicken, sausages and burgers as a camp fire burned to the accompaniment of music from Paul McCartney and Wings' album, Band on the Run. Over £7,000 was raised for the local community and a large fibreglass reindeer that 'went missing' from the event was returned with no questions asked.

Billy's purchases from auctions at the time weren't restricted to furniture for Stranocum Hall. He says: "I also bought rare bottles of liquor including a 300th anniversary bottle of whiskey that commemorated the Battle of the Boyne and a collection of military items including German and Italian rifles from the gun-running ship, the Clyde Valley including UVF badges from the North Irish Bar and McLarnons restaurant in Dervock.

The O'Neills' reputation for playing host to charity functions was spreading and in the autumn the couple were approached by Mr. and Mrs. Leslie of Leslie Hill to have a fund raising event for the National Society for the Prevention of Cruelty to Children whose chairperson was Lady Moyra Campbell who was one of the Queen's six maids of honour at her wedding. The function at Stranocum Hall was another triumph but the weather, according to Billy, was dreadful.

The next function was a more personal affair, a combined house-warming celebration and a party for Billy's 60th birthday. The first part of the evening was a meal in the house that was nearly complete for living in followed by a knees-up in the barn with Plug and Dominic providing the music and the food supplied by Ernest Bustard, Flash Outside Catering.

Lady Moyra Campbell former NI Chairperson NSPCC

Billy's passion for collectables had, however, almost landed him in trouble. He'd bought a number of statues at Wilson's Auctions at Mallusk including one of a hanged man and another 12 of mannequins of ladies which he took back to Stranocum in the back of large trailer.

The wind however blew part of the canvas covering off the mannequins and passing motorists who were alarmed by what they saw alerted the PSNI who stopped Billy near Dunloy but luckily saw the funny side of it all.

Billy also raised a laugh at the house-warming as he re-created a scene involving a wake for the former owner of the house George 'Bloody' Hutchinson who had been responsible for the execution of a number of members of the United Irishmen who attempted a revolution in 1798.

Billy explains: "I'd bought a plastic skull with a mouse looking out of one eye and a spider in the other and a battery operated hand inside the sleeve of a United Irishman's 18th century uniform that moved when someone made a noise.

"Later one of the guests who'd had a fair bit of drink tried to chat up one of the mannequins who had been dressed up to the nines including a fur coat and a fox head stole. It was only after his fiancée led him away that the amorous man realised the subject of his affections wasn't real."

On a more serious point Billy made an emotional speech on his 60th on behalf of Lily and his sons welcoming the guests and thanking everyone who had made the night possible.

He also remembered absent friends like the hypnotist Edwin Heath who had died in January 1999 not long after he and his wife Margaret celebrated the O'Neills' first New Year's Eve with them at Stranocum.

Intriguingly as the birthday party drew to a close some of the guests wanted to investigate rumours that they'd heard about the ghost of 'a grey lady' who was said to have roamed the cellar kitchen at Stranocum Hall after 3am to help prepare the breakfast for the gentry of the house. "Lily wanted to meet her to let her know that she was the boss of Stranocum Hall now. But the grey lady didn't appear," laughs Billy who soon afterwards spotted an amusing present for his wife at Wilson's Auctions. "I was amazed to see titles for sale by an archery organisation called the Company of the Plantagenet Toxophilites and Lily was declared Dame Elizabeth Grace O'Neill of the Long Bow while I became Sir William Weir O'Neill of the Long Bow. But the thing is we have never used the titles once in over 22 years."

17

Michael Jackson, Mick Jagger and Stephen Nolan

Billy and Lily soon found themselves sitting at Stranocum in the very same chairs that musical megastar Michael Jackson had once relaxed in. That's because they bought furniture that came from an Irish fairytale castle which was a retreat for Michael Jackson for three months in 2005/06 when he paid 30,000 euro a week for the privilege of the privacy not long after he had been acquitted on charges in America. A Regency suite from the Guinness family's estate at Luggala Castle in County Wicklow came up for auction and the O'Neills bought it.

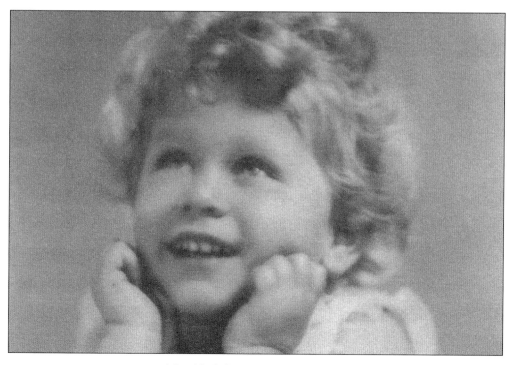

A Royal Smile from HRH Princess Elizabeth

The suite, consisting of three and four seat settees and two armchairs, had originally been in the one-time home of the former revolutionary Countess Markievicz, Lissadell House in County Sligo where WB Yeats, Mick Jagger and Marianne Faithful were listed among the guests down through the years.

"The suite suited the house but it wasn't very comfortable," says Billy. "I should have kept the leather one we had."

The gathering together of more furniture was going well at auctions including a collection from the home of a judge in Dublin who had once been robbed by the notorious gangster Martin 'The General' Cahill who was the subject of a movie starring Brendan Gleason.

Billy also bought a desk that had been owned by Judge Lancelot Curran whose 19 year old daughter Patricia was murdered in 1952 at Whiteabbey, a tragedy that gripped Northern Ireland for decades.

Billy also purchased fireguards, tables, paintings and drawings of old Coleraine and Ballycastle that he still cherishes.

A music cabinet revealed a secret drawer in which a photograph was found of an Army officer which Billy was able to send to a family member of the soldier that he tracked down.

Another photo in a sweet bag that Billy initially thought was of the child star Shirley Temple was later confirmed – after he put his glasses on – to be of a very young Princess Elizabeth who later became Queen.

The O'Neills were soon attracting media attention with their renovations at Stranocum Hall. A four page spread appeared in Home Magazine and shortly afterwards Billy and Lily received a letter all the way from Australia from a man called Richard John Sinclair Hutchinson, a descendant of the family who had built the house. A family tree was also enclosed by Mr Hutchinson whose son Peter visited Stranocum Hall some time later.

Billy's fervour for collecting saw him buying pewter mugs and teapots initially for the Dunluce room in his hotel but he soon had over 500 pieces which are now in the garage of his home in Portstewart.

The garage is a quite remarkable sight and also includes a huge number of car registration plates from around the world, mostly from America.

With over 400 adverts and pictures of movie stars, the old Giant's Causeway tram and Ballymoney as well as photos of vintage cars plus horse brasses there's barely an inch of space left free on the walls of the garage.

In 2000 Stranocum Hall was the focus of a BBC programme called The Right Move. The interviewer was Stephen Nolan and the idea was to show how the O'Neills had swapped a hotel for a country house.

Lily and Billy were wary. They'd seen Nolan in action and feared he might give them a hard time. However they agreed to allow the filming to go ahead and with the connivance of the crew Billy played a trick on Nolan getting a huge model of a spider to fall down on him from a height.

The fright didn't deter the presenter and the team captured the essence of Stranocum Hall, the barn, the Coachman's House and cobbled yard with its collection of antique farm implements including a manure spreader, horse drawn ploughs and a re-creation of a blacksmith's forge.

"Stephen had a lot of questions for us. He was trying to make Lily say that I was crazy, but she was well able for him and we all had two good days of fun and laughter," says Billy who had added a collection of taxidermy to Stranocum after buying it at Mealy's auctions.

The Irish elk skulls, a walrus head, a full size leopard and a huge brown bear some of which had been rented out in the past to film producers were just a few of the 'animals' in the barn. And Billy placed the bear in an old pulpit to represent a preacher delivering a sermon.

An old clerical friend came back into the O'Neills lives in September 2001 when Billy and Lily celebrated their 40th wedding anniversary in style.

The Fleet

Fr Langan who had married the couple in Glasgow officiated at a ceremony in Dervock where they renewed their vows in front of family and friends at the Church of Our Lady and St John the Evangelist where Billy's parents had been wed.

The local newspapers covered the O'Neills' renewal of their vows but one writer said the church ceremony 'paled' compared to the celebrations at Stranocum Hall afterwards.

The article said: "Members of the Living History Department of the Palace Studios in Armagh transported guests back to 1766 when the estate was owned by the Hutchinson family"

Actors brought back to life the characters from the old Hall including a nobleman and three servant girls who mingled with guests at the reception. One paper said: "The touch of living history transformed the occasion from the norm to the extraordinary" A footnote to the article revealed the little known fact that Fr Langan had lost six members of his family in the Lockerbie disaster in December 1988 when a Libyan bomb exploded on a US-bound plane over the Scottish village, killing 259 passengers and crew on board and 11 Scots on the ground.

A letter that Billy and Lily received on May 7, 2002 was priceless to them. It came from the Northern Ireland Office inviting them to meet the Queen and the Duke of Edinburgh at a garden party at Hillsborough Castle to mark the 50th anniversary of the monarch coming to the throne. The O'Neills who had been to Buckingham Palace for a garden party but didn't actually meet the Royals accepted the invitation and their Golden Jubilee day was one they never forgot.

At the start of the following year the O'Neills added a new house to their portfolio but not one in Northern Ireland. They decided that a holiday home in Fort Myers, Florida would be perfect for the whole family, with Billy and Lily visiting it for three or four months a year and Terry and Stephen and their families going there as well.

18

The dancehall sweethearts and a ten from Len Goodman

T he TV cameras were back again to film Billy and Lily nine years after their encounter with Stephen Nolan and this time the couple were in the spotlight for their dancing. The producers of Dancehall Sweethearts, presented by Newtownards' Christine Bleakley targeted people who had fallen in love in places like the Arcadia Ballroom which was, of course, where Billy and Lily met many years earlier. The three-part series which aired in April 2009 was a huge hit with the viewers who remembered dancing and romancing in venues like the Plaza and the Floral Hall in Belfast as well as the Arcadia.

Strictly Len

Fast forward ten years to the time of the staging of the Open golf championship in Portrush where the BBC filmed a series of specials from the North Coast, one of them called Dancehall Sweethearts, featured the Arcadia.

The presenter this time was a hero of the O'Neills, Len Goodman who was a judge on the enormously popular Strictly Come Dancing blockbuster TV show.

Producer Jackie Adair set up a preliminary meeting between the O'Neills and Len and they all hit it off, so much so that the Englishman autographed a photo for Lily and Billy with his TV catchphrase: "You're a ten from Len."

Billy and Lily appeared in front of the cameras in the Arcadia dressed in the sort of gear that would have been worn by dancers in the 50s.

The couple also gave a demonstration of the way they danced 60 years earlier.

But Billy says: "It was a lot slower than the old days. A group of younger people were dressed in the 50s style and they danced in the ballroom. Sadly my own Teddy Boy suits were long gone."

Len and Billy reminisced about going to the world rock and roll dance contest in the Lyceum ballroom on London's Strand where the BBC's popular TV series Come Dancing was staged. The two men also discovered they had also shared a fondness for the same dance halls in the English capital.

Len asked Billy if he remembered the first time he had ever seen Lily and of course he did. He was able to recall the exact details of where he was in the Arcadia, what soft drink he was sipping and what Lily was wearing. Len asked Billy what his epitaph would be and he said: "I told him it used to be 'you ain't got a thing if you ain't got that swing. But I joked that I was thinking of changing it to 'if there's no dancing in Heaven I am not going.'

The importance of the Arcadia to Billy and Lily is underlined by the fact that on the wall of their home they have a huge framed history of the ballroom with a large number of photographs of the much cherished building overlooking the Atlantic ocean.

It was built in the 1920s by local businessman R.A Chalmers and was originally designed as a café but opened its ballroom in 1953. The Arcadia didn't only play host to showbands like Dave Glover's outfit down the years, it also welcomed more unconventional pop groups like The Stranglers, The Undertones, Stiff Little Fingers and Ian Dury and the Blockheads.

The O'Neills' history records that the main ballroom was demolished in the 1990s and that the adjoining building risked the same fate until Portrush residents rallied round and the surviving section of the Arcadia was restored in the early 2000s. It's now a café and exhibition space and the site of the old ballroom has been transformed into a children's play area.

One of the photos on the O'Neills' wall shows that in the 1890s a beach hut stood where the Arcadia was later built. Alongside the homage to the Arcadia in the O'Neills' home there's another framed display reflecting Billy and Lily's passion for music and dancing.

Entitled 'The Rock and Roll Era' it includes a series of pictures showing the couple strutting their stuff on dance floors near and far.

It also features a potted written history of their dancing career and calls Billy 'a dedicated Teddy Boy' who loved living and working in the Medway in England as a teenager from 1956 because it was 'a great place to have suits made.'

It also quotes Billy as saying he worked hard across the water to save money to buy his first Teddy Boy suit and adds him saying of the time: "There's Teddy Boys and there's Teddy Boys...those who just hung about on street corners and did nothing and those who were serious about it."

The article also recounts how he and Lily met at the Arcadia and how they would dance six nights a week there. Billy and Lily's dancing was also to feature in the Daily Mail. In the paper's Questions and Answers section a reader had asked if anyone recalled a Sixties craze for skip jiving.

Billy wrote back that in his time living in Rochester, Kent working at the Isle of Grain BP oil refinery for four years he and friends frequented jazz clubs and dance halls in the Medway towns, plus London.

He said: "We had many great nights jiving with local girls Brenda Cummings, Jean Connelly, Christine Bannfield and others whose names I don't recall." Billy reminisced about one all-night event in the Albert Hall in London where 14 top jazz bands were on the bill including George Melly. "We jived, skip jived and jitterbugged," he said, adding that he was still jiving!

The Daily Mail featured pictures of Billy dancing with Brenda Cummings in the Star Ballroom, Maidstone in 1958 alongside another photograph of him jiving with his wife Lily in the Sixties.

Away from the limelight, Billy wasn't finished with his Stranocum Hall project even though he was forging ahead with his developments in Ballymoney and Portstewart.

At yet another auction he bought a 90ft x 50ft plant tunnel that he thought would make a permanent marquee and it was erected near the barn. Billy was extremely pleased with how the barn looked with its quirky extras including a confession box for a telephone kiosk and creamery cans with tractor seats on them. It was, he reckoned, the perfect setting for even more charity events like the Masonic barbecue that had 800 guests and raised £4,500 for a charity trying to raise awareness of diabetes. Highlighting all the good causes that the O'Neill's helped over a 50 year period is truly breath-taking and the charities that benefitted from their largesse are listed later on in this book. At the last count it was estimated that down the years Billy and Lily played a part in raising a staggering £230,000 – at least - for their charities and no fewer than 35 barbecues were hosted by them at Stranocum. As yet however no-one has even attempted to guess how many burgers and chicken pieces were scoffed by the thousands of guests!

Ballymoney Rotary Club, charity breakfast

Billy president Coleraine Lions Club

The Rotary Club Of Ballymoney

COUNTRY & WESTERN JAMBOREE

Lend a Hand

Saturday 24 April - 8.30 PM
Stranocum Hall
Music by - Band On The Run
Special Guest - Fiddler Adam
Line Dancing Demonstration
Admission: £12.50 (including Knife & Fork Supper)
All proceeds to Rotary International Charities

Marquee set for 250 wedding guests

With the reputation of Stranocum Hall spreading in the newspapers and by word of mouth, it was hardly surprising that the O'Neills received more and more requests to open up the magnificent estate to visitors.

Billy says Keith Beattie, the manager of Ballymoney Museum, was a huge help to him in his research into the history of Stranocum Hall.

The late Dalriada schoolteacher and historian, Alex Blair, who was a fine raconteur and actor, was drafted in to be a guide on a number of tours to Stranocum. And his in-depth knowledge of the history of the Hall and its surroundings certainly enlivened the visits with the proceeds going to the NSPCC and Cancer Research charities.

On one coach tour a guest asked Billy to tell her what he would save first from the Hall in the event of a fire. "I had no hesitation in saying it would be my wife Lily "says Billy who was later informed by insurers that he wasn't allowed to have viewing upstairs at Stranocum because there was no fire escape. The bottom line was that it also made the cost of insurance to cover any functions very high.

Ballymoney Museum

19

Attempts to lease new caravan sites are scuppered

Back on the north coast a major development about caravan parks between Portrush and Portstewart caused a stir in 2005 and caught the eye of Billy O'Neill and his family. Coleraine Borough Council (CBC) announced that they were planning to lease the massive Carrick Dhu and Juniper Hill sites to private companies to run instead of the local authority.

Carrick Dhu

A spokeswoman from CBC told the Belfast Telegraph that following a review of the caravan park operation, the council had decided to investigate the leasing option but that no decision had yet been made about the future operation of Juniper Hill and Carrick Dhu. She added: "However, we would stress that the council have agreed that these areas must continue to operate as caravan parks and any prospective lease must agree to operate the parks under current codes of practice agreed between the Office of Fair Trading and the National Caravan Council, thus protecting current site holders." Billy says that he had read in the press several years earlier that the council had had a review of caravan park provision and in their 'final report' they had concluded that it was evident they were not geared up to maximise the full return of their 'valuable assets' at Juniper Hill and Carrick Dhu. Billy says the council report added: "Within the constraints of the public sector- not least an inability to trade- it is not possible to emulate the standards of service and response similar to those now operated by the private sector parks. This coupled with the need for major investment makes leasing the preferred option."

A brief history in a brochure showed that Carrick Dhu and Juniper Hill had been established in the 1960s by the former Londonderry County Council 'to bring some order to the proliferation of old shacks and caravans sited off the main A2 road between Portrush and Portstewart.' It continued: "These unofficial sites were without proper water and sewage facilities and constituted a major health hazard as well as being a blight on the landscape of an area of beauty. The new sites were operated by Londonderry County Council until 1973." In that year the re-organisation of local government saw the two sites being transferred into the ownership of CBC who had managed them since that time, with the council saying the parks had proved 'extremely popular' with both static and touring caravanners over the years. But the council said: "With the tremendous increase in the number of privately owned caravan parks in Northern Ireland in general, and the Causeway Coast area in particular, Council are now operating in an extremely competitive commercial environment and now wish to review the operation of both parks and consider all options for the future." A number of caravanners were reported to be furious with the proposals for leasing the parks and claimed they had not been consulted by CBC and vowed to fight any changes with an SOS campaign, standing for Save Our Sites.

The protesting caravanners said they believed if the parks were privatised, they would be faced with new terms and conditions which would mean the majority of people who used them would no longer be able to afford to keep a caravan. O'Neills' Caravans and the family's other associated company Bonalston Caravans were, like every other company of their ilk, interested in bidding for the contracts but Billy had had initial reservations because of the shortness of the leases that were on offer. He insisted he wouldn't be making a bid for anything less than a 50 year lease which was subsequently upped to 99 years.

On October 27 Billy submitted an 'expression of interest form' for what was described as the leasehold purchase of the Carrick Dhu and Juniper Hill. He put in written financial offers for the leaseholds along with a letter from the Bank confirming their intention to support the application which also included a detailed analysis and history of the O'Neills' involvement in the operation of caravan parks in Northern Ireland. The council's chartered surveyors quickly informed Billy that he had been shortlisted for the next stage of the leasing process, inviting him to an interview on November 17 at CBC offices in

Coleraine. A letter informed him that three other parties had been shortlisted to meet an interview panel consisting of selected councillors, council officers and professional advisors who formed part of the 'Caravan Park Working Group.'

The application by the O'Neills – backed by a 14 page dossier – contained their proposals on how to run the two caravan parks and how the firm intended to bring what they acknowledged were well-maintained and attractive amenities to five-star standard. Their plans included making the caravan parks more modern and more attractive; improving security with automated gates, requiring a key card for access and better lighting; and upgrading safety measures in relation to traffic as well as the installation of cycle paths plus ways of encouraging owners to use their caravans in the low season as well as the peak summer months.

The dossier also outlined a brief background on the O'Neills' caravans operations and Bonalston Caravans Ltd who were jointly bidding for the new leases at Carrick Dhu and Juniper Hill. The submission said that while the Bonalston company - run by the O'Neills' sons Terry and Stephen - was financially separate from O'Neills' Caravans the two companies were 'inextricably linked through family bonds with much of the management, development and business planning shared.'

It revealed how Bonalston was formed in 1984 with the purchase of Castlerock Holiday Park which had it said been extensively developed and extended to provide Castlerock with a 'sought after Northern Ireland Tourist Board four star graded tourist facility incorporating an area of first class modern three bedroom centrally heated and double-glazed caravans for hire.'

The dossier said Bonalston expanded its interests by purchasing Millfield Holiday Village in Portstewart, adding: "The park lay out was redesigned and now enjoys full occupancy with a waiting list of people wanting to come on. Later in 2000 the company was successful in securing the purchase of Ballyleese Town and Country Caravan Park, Portstewart along with 70 acres of adjoining land in 2001. This park is now graded five star by NITB. When ownership was handed over there were only three caravans sited, now it also enjoys full occupancy and has a waiting list."

The application for the Carrick Dhu and Juniper Hill leases was supported by a presentation by Billy's son Terry giving an overview on their plans for the Council Parks and the companies' achievements in running five caravan parks in the province. The interviews duly went ahead but a major controversy erupted not long afterwards after financial details of Billy's proposals for the leasing and development of the Carrick Dhu and Juniper Hill caravan parks appeared in the local press. Billy wrote to the council's Town Clerk and Chief Executive Wavell T.Moore on January 18, 2006 to protest. He said: "Given that I understood all matters relating to the leasing arrangements were to be carried out in a confidential manner, I am aghast that details of my proposals presented on 'a commercial-in-confidence' basis at a council meeting – IN COMMITTEE – are now in the public domain and could be damaging to my position. As such could you please inform me how this confidential information was 'leaked' to the press? I find this all the more alarming given that in our participation in this competition we were required to sign a confidentiality clause." Billy added that he believed that follow-up proposals from other interested parties in subsequent meetings could be influenced by the fact that they had had sight of his offer. In an article in the Coleraine Times in advance of another meeting, a Sinn Fein councillor, Billy Leonard went on the attack, saying that confidentiality in CBC 'means nothing.' The report continued: "He (Cllr Leonard) was referring to discussions over the possible leasing of the council owned Carrick Dhu and Juniper Hill caravan parks. Councillor Leonard claimed 'that specific details from a so-called private meeting' about the caravan parks were now out among many caravanners adding: "I have been given information from several sources that the name of one operator who expressed interest in leasing the sites has been shared by a councillor. It is incredible to think that information from a closed council meeting is talked about openly by a councillor. And I wonder if this has now compromised the process. There was a place for these confidential meetings to study the detail but I am already on record as saying that the process should be brought into the open. I therefore strongly disagree with the decision to have Friday's meeting behind closed doors. This is particularly unfair on the caravanners but it is not good for the whole ethos of openness and transparency as we reach decision stage. The public at large deserve openness as councillors rationalise their vote on the biggest financial decision we face in this council term. The Coleraine Times contacted Coleraine Borough Council but they refused to comment further on the issue." In a letter dated February 13, 2006 Mr Moore acknowledged that 'certain financial information' within Billy's proposal had come into the public domain despite councillors and officials being told it was 'strictly confidential.' He added: "I have already made it clear to members that the leaking of such information is totally reprehensible and extremely unhelpful. However beyond that admonition I have no statutory powers to regulate members' actions in this regard. I am further quite satisfied that no officer of Council was responsible for the leaking of this information." Mr Moore also said that he was satisfied that Billy's firm had not been commercially disadvantaged by the unauthorised disclosures. The letter further confirmed that CBC had now decided not to lease the caravan parks but rather to retain the management of both of them 'in-house.'

Mr Moore said that he could understand Billy's disappointment with the outcome, adding: "This decision came at the end of a comprehensive exercise by Council which involved market testing the option of leasing the operation of both parks. Throughout all of this exercise I am satisfied that the approach has been both professional and transparent."

Billy is prepared to reveal now that the offer he made was for £9.1 million (almost double what the runner-up was offering) and the word among people in the know was that his bid had been successful. But things didn't quite work out that way. It was later reported that a council committee meeting in the Cloonavin headquarters went to a vote on whether or not the leases to the two caravan parks should be sold. In the end the council decided not to do so. Billy says he was bitterly disappointed by the outcome. Some caravan owners were shocked. One wrote to the newspapers saying: "Having taken almost 18 months to make a decision, the council has "after very careful deliberation" finally come to the conclusion that it will retain the operation and management of both parks."

20

Doing it their way in Frank Sinatra's old place

T aking themselves well away from Northern Ireland for a family break in 1996, it
was ironic that the O'Neills, who were so closely associated with the holiday
and tourism business through their caravan parks and other developments in
Northern Ireland, should find themselves in a hotel once used by Oul Blues Eyes,
Frank Sinatra. The Cal Neva resort on the border of Nevada and California at Lake
Tahoe was the spectacular location for the wedding of Billy and Lily's son Terry and
his partner Stephanie (Stevie) Kelly.

The Queen pins medal on Billy

Billy and Lily at the Palace

Billy was fascinated with the history of the place which was where the legendary Rat Pack – Sinatra, Dean Martin, Peter Lawford and Sammy Davis Jr. regularly hung out with other stars like the glamorous Marilyn Monroe.

The wedding ceremony in one of the Cal Neva's lodges was memorable and Billy says that after a few libations several of the guests including Terry and Kevin O'Malley, still wearing their tuxedos, went for a swim in a hotel pool, part of which was in Nevada and the other in California.

After the 'amazing' wedding festivities the O'Neills and their friends and relatives did a lot of exploring in the old silver mines around Nevada and enjoying famous bars like the Bucket of Blood which had a horse drawn hearse outside it.

The O'Neills' own mode of transport back home in Northern Ireland was somewhat different. Billy who'd graduated from a cheap bike to the splendour of a Bentley reckoned it was time for an upgrade in the luxury car stakes.

After driving a 16 year old Bentley turbo car he decided a new one wouldn't be overdue and to celebrate his and Lily's wedding anniversary he had a test drive of a new Bentley Continental Flying Spur at Charles Hurst showrooms.

He liked what he saw and placed an order for the Flying Spur for a delivery four months later. To his surprise he was invited to see the car being built at Bentley's base in Crewe, England.

"That was an experience in itself, "says Billy. "The factory was as clean as a hospital. The assembly workers were wearing white coats and the women preparing the wood for the dash boards and the seats were dressed like nurses. I was shown videos of the technology side of the vehicle but the real treat I got was at the finishing room where the Queen's new special height dark purple Bentley was sitting.

"I got to sit behind the steering wheel for two minutes and it was also a thrill to see the white Bentleys sitting in a row waiting for delivery to customers in Arab countries."

Billy took delivery of the new Bentley just before the wedding anniversary and his first trip in it was to a Rotary Club rally in Dublin.

Lily told Billy she would like him to buy her something new, something that was lower to the ground and went from 0-120 in 2 seconds. "I bought her a set of bathroom scales," says Billy who was relieved that his wife saw the funny side of his gesture.

A more substantial purchase came at the start of 2007 when Billy ventured into a new part of Northern Ireland to buy a caravan park. He'd been contacted by estate agent Tony O'Connor from the property agents O'Connor, Kennedy Turtle to say he had been approached to sell a park in Minerstown near Tyrella Beach in County Down. "I knew the owner was emigrating to South Africa, " says Billy. "And I did a deal through OKT and I took on my nephew Loren as a partner. He and his family who had been living in the gate lodge at Stranocum were interested in the caravan business and at the end of February they

Terry and Stephen with Mum and Dad

Billy receiving his MBE from the Queen

started to manage the new park which is now called The Edgewater Holiday Park. I have now sold my share of the park to Loren and his family."

All the while The O'Neills were still helping to raise large sums of money for charities.

Billy became President of Ballymoney Rotary Club and enthusiastically fulfilled his duties across the UK and on his holidays in Florida he made 12 visits to three different clubs in the Fort Myers area.

On a trip nearer home to Bournemouth for a Rotary Club function in April 2007 Lily took seriously ill and needed an operation for bowel cancer on her return to Northern Ireland.

The surgery was declared a success and there was another fillip for the O'Neills shortly afterwards when Billy received news that he was being awarded an MBE. "My mother-in-law was living with us at the time and she asked me what I was getting it for and I joked that it was a reward for marrying her daughter. It was said that I was Sally's favourite son-in-law but truth to tell I was her only one! I also said that behind every successful man stands a surprised mother-in-law, " laughs Billy who was delighted that Lily shared his elation at his Royal honour which a citation said was for his services to the community.

"I initially thought I was getting the MBE for what I had done for tourism but then I found out that it was for what I had contributed to the community," adds Billy.

Billy says his Presidential year in the Rotary Club was full of highlights including fund raising for charities and talks from visiting dignitaries including Cecil Graham LVO OBE who spoke about the work of the Prince's Trust

In the middle of the year, in July 2007 Lily's aforementioned bathroom scales were replaced with a new Lexus car by Billy who organised a family trip in London for October 23 when he was due to collect his MBE at Buckingham Palace from the Queen.

Billy took Lily, Terry and Stephen to the Palace with him to see the ceremony and they got seats in the Royal ballroom in the second row.

Proud as punch Billy recalls: "I was directed to a long room like an art gallery with about 60 or 70 other recipients who were all looking to see if there were any recognisable celebrities in our midst. Eventually we were lined up to receive our medals from the Queen who was very well informed about the reason that I received the award of the MBE."

The monarch also inquired how long Billy had been in business and when he replied 36 years she said: "Very good." Official photographers took pictures of the honourees who included a number of people who received knighthoods.

The Coleraine Chronicle was just one of a number of local newspapers that reported Billy's visit to London in depth alongside the photographs outside the Palace.

An article said that Billy's honour was recognition for his support for a vast array of good causes not least his commitment to the Northern Ireland Milk Cup football tournament and for his work to bolster the local community with charity initiatives on his own behalf and with the Lions Club and the Rotary Club.

The report also talked of Billy's 'famed generosity that facilitated many charities and community groups at his stunning home Stranocum Hall.' The article said that Billy had endeared himself to many people and turning to the future it added that the businessman showed no signs of slowing down despite his advancing years. It went on: "While he may have passed the reins of most of his business interests to his two sons he still retains a keen interest in future developments." The report quoted Billy as saying: "We are currently building houses on the site of a former caravan park in Portstewart while I also have plans for future developments in Ballymoney."

In London after the investiture the wives of the O'Neill boys were waiting outside the palace along with Billy's brother Hughie and they all retired to the renowned Reubens Hotel for lunch and took in a show, Chicago, in the West End.

Billy says: "That visit to London to receive my MBE was a wonderful highpoint in my life which would never have happened if it hadn't been for the backing from Lily and my family and from good friends over the years."

Billy didn't linger long in London because he had a very important function to attend back home in Northern Ireland - a dinner to raise money to erect a statue of the legendary Coleraine, Celtic and Northern Ireland football legend, Bertie Peacock in Coleraine's Diamond.

Billy's father Ned had been friends with the Peacock family dating back to the war and his sons were pals with Bertie's cousins.

However Billy says he didn't really get to know Bertie Peacock until he and the chairman of the fledgling Milk Cup competition Victor Leonard approached him to rent all the chalets in his Holiday Park in Portstewart to accommodate the visiting young footballers.

The latter part of 2007 marked another red-letter date in the Billy and Lily O'Neill story. On a QE2 cruise to the Canary Islands a priest from County Wexford let it be known that he would renew the wedding vows of any couples who wanted him to do so.

Billy and Lily were in their 46th year of marriage and decided to exchange their vows with their close friends Sammy and Niki Moore acting as best man and bridesmaid again.

Sadly however over the next few years Billy and Lily lost a number of people who were close, and dear to them.

Lily Rohdich, a one-time assistant to hypnotist Edwin Heath, had been a dancing friend for 40 years and her husband Albert gave her a musical send-off. After Requiem Mass he organised a dinner – and a jazz band - in the Parochial Hall in Portrush which had formerly been the Palladium ballroom.

Another shock came with the news that Billy's brother Hughie died after having what was thought would be a routine heart operation in a London hospital. His passing was a shattering blow for Billy who had so many happy memories of living with Hughie and his wife Joan for four years in Rochester from the age of 16 to 20. After Hughie's cremation in Medway his ashes were scattered around a tree which was just a few hundred yards from where the two brothers had shared their first caravan in the spring of 1962.

Just after the funeral Billy paid a visit to the grave in Rainham, Kent of another brother, James who had worked alongside Hughie. Billy was to come back down to earth – literally- some time later. After a CLIC Sergeant charity country and western music jamboree and barbecue which raised nearly £3000 in June 2008 for young people with cancer in Northern Ireland Billy took a tumble at Stranocum when he was down in the cellar.

Billy says: "It was dark and I missed the last step. I heard a crack but I didn't know how much damage I had done. The next morning my knee was very sore and my niece Bernadette drove me to the Causeway hospital in Coleraine. Quite incredibly I was asked there if I was a hypochondriac. I was told by a doctor that an X-ray showed that the knee wasn't broken and I was sent home in agony.

"I took painkillers and tried to sleep but the pain persisted and the knee kept swelling up to the point where I simply couldn't bear it and after a couple of days I went back to the hospital where after another X-ray the same doctor from the previous visit agreed that my knee was broken.

"Having broken my right tibia and fibula when I was 20 and then when I was 27 I realised the latest injury would take time to mend. I knew that yet again I wouldn't be dancing for a while."

In that summer of 2008 however Billy was still able to come to the rescue of the prestigious Milk Cup competition on the North Coast.

Coleraine-born journalist Grant Cameron was all across the story on July 4, 2008. He wrote that the Milk Cup would cost a staggering £265,000 to stage that year 'with its army of volunteer organisers facing their toughest test yet to come up with the ready cash.'

Grant questioned why the Irish Football Association who he said were supposed to promote the game here had voted earlier in 2008 to withdraw their annual grant to the tournament through the Sports Council.

But Grant's column continued: "It wasn't the end of the world for the professional behind-the-scenes committee members of the Milk Cup which was to be officially opened by Welsh international team manager and ex-Manchester United legend Mark Hughes after the traditional parade of teams to Coleraine Showgrounds tomorrow morning. They simply knuckled down and worked harder to make up the shortfall. And they found a knight in shining armour in the shape of one generous but most irate North Coast businessman. Tournament chairman Victor Leonard takes up the story: "When news broke of the IFA's decision to deny us funds, we had many calls from worried supporters who thought the competition was about to go under. That was never going to happen but the loss of an annual grant certainly didn't make our job any easier. However a good friend of the tournament, Billy O'Neill, contacted me to offer help. Up until last year we had used Billy's former hotel on the coast between Portrush and Portstewart as our base. Billy very kindly made a donation which helped us out of a hole and we are all grateful to him."

Ballyleese Town & Country Caravan Park

Ballyness Caravan Park

Harry Staddon standing on left in Bushmills Youth Club teaching PE

21

A break-in at Stranocum opens up a move to Portstewart

Living in Stranocum Hall took a major downturn for Billy and Lily on August 5,2010. An intruder broke into the property during the night but Lily and Billy didn't know about it until Francis Stuart who cut the grass and had a key so that he could look after the property when the O'Neills were away, told them. Francis had come into the house carrying antique guns, swords a helmet and other items which he had found lying outside but couldn't immediately work out why they were there. In the front room a cracked window was discovered and downstairs in the cellar another window was open, leaving no room for doubt that a burglar had broken in while Billy

Ocean Green, Ocean Drive

and Lily were sleeping in their bed. "It was a horrible feeling," says Billy who called the police.

Billy later watched three hours of CCTV footage and was able to see a lone intruder in a black balaclava shining a torch through a conservatory window around 3.30am before gaining access to the dining room, taking his time to root through papers before putting a number of items into a rucksack.

Billy says the man stared at the security cameras as if he knew they were there.

Chillingly the intruder was still inside Stranocum Hall three hours after he broke in and at one point he actually took time to answer a call on his mobile phone.

Reports at the time said that a number of other houses in the area were also burgled but no-one was ever arrested.

Billy carefully studied tapes that had been made of Stranocum Hall by his nephew to identify what had been stolen but the O'Neills were left unsettled by the burglary.

"It drastically changed our view about living in an isolated area, "says Billy who was told by police that it had been fortunate that neither he nor Lily had been disturbed by their intruder because things might have been worse if there had been a confrontation. "

The decision was made to sell Stranocum Hall and it was heavily influenced by the robbery.

The gate lodge sold quickly but the main house proved harder to sell. However when a new buyer was found, the news made headlines in the local press.

A report in the Belfast Telegraph compared Stranocum Hall to Downton Abbey the stately home in the incredibly popular TV series of that name. Downton was, of course, a fictional abode and the dramas were actually filmed in Highclere Castle in Hampshire.

The Belfast Telegraph article about the sale of Stranocum Hall read: "You could have just about acquired a well-located apartment in Belfast for £350,000 at the height of the property boom. But, yesterday, one lucky buyer walked away with one of Northern Ireland's finest Georgian country residences for significantly less than that.

Stranocum Hall - a magnificent Downton Abbey-style stately home in Co Antrim - was sold at auction for £307,500. It was one of 50 properties and land that went under the hammer in two hours at Belfast's Europa Hotel, generating sales in excess of £3m. Chartered surveyor Ian Harbinson, who is also an associate director at Lambert Smith Hampton (LSH), said it was the catch of the day, "Getting Stranocum Hall for just £7,500 over the asking price was definitely a huge bargain," he added. "That property would have been worth double in 2007, and I doubt you could build it for £310,000 today."Top of Form Bottom of Form The article continued: "The fine Georgian residence is one of the most splendid properties in Co Antrim.Its elevated rural setting, a short distance from the village, provides uninterrupted views over the River Bush valley and miles of surrounding countryside. Situated on Fivey Road, Stranocum Hall was fully restored 17 years ago, and also benefits from the possibility of using the coachman's house as a detached residence. Mr Harbinson added that it was one of the most impressive offerings LSH had brought to

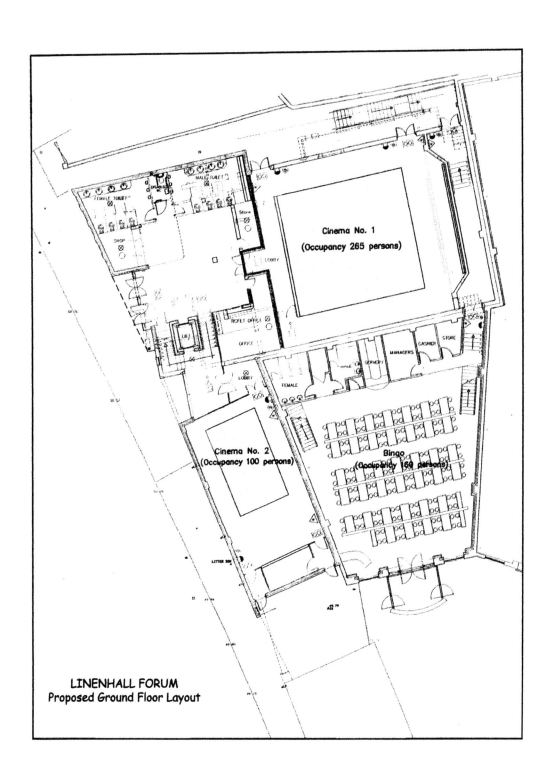

Cinema No. 1
(Occupancy 265 persons)

Cinema No. 2
(Occupancy 100 persons)

Bingo
(Occupancy 150 persons)

LINENHALL FORUM
Proposed Ground Floor Layout

auction to date. More than 300 people turned up yesterday to see 37 successful property and land deals raise a collective £3,314,600."

Billy and Lily's achievements in saving Stranocum Hall have been widely recognised including in the Northern Ireland Community Forum Archive. It features before and after pictures of the Hall, firstly one in its dilapidated, ruinous state and then one of the building that had been lovingly restored by Billy and Lily for whom it was a wrench to leave their home at Stranocum. (The Community Forum Archive, coincidentally, also includes other pictures which are close to Billy's heart. For they show the Rodden Foot as it was in Billy's younger days, with a row of terraced single storey houses and another row of two up two down houses like the one at number 16 in which the O'Neills lived.) But even before selling up Billy and Lily had, for some time, been thinking about building a retirement home for themselves in the popular seaside town of Portstewart. The opportunity presented itself after Billy finally received planning permission for a new development at Burnside Caravan Park. A builder was enlisted to construct a mixture of 16 houses and apartments overlooking Portstewart Strand the golf course and the historic Mussenden Temple in the distance beyond Castlerock. One of the houses, Billy and Lily decided, would be the ideal place for them to live in retirement. Seventeen caravans were moved from Burnside road to Ballyleese Town and Country Park to make way for the new development.

The uptake on the new dwellings on what became known as Ocean Drive was encouraging with many ex-pats snapping them up as retirement homes just as Billy and Lily had done. After the move to Ocean Drive in March 2017 Billy had a two day auction at Stranocum Hall conducted by Richard Bell from Wilson's Auctions with most of the items up for bidding, farm machinery, military memorabilia including uniforms, and taxidermy. Billy's cast-iron seat collection went under the hammer at a specialised auction in England and large pieces of furniture were sold at a three-day auction at Mealy's in Castlecomer in March 2015.

Billy says he got a return on his investments from his 44 years of collecting but he kept hold of many of his favourite things, many of which are displayed around their new home, parts of which are akin to a museum.

Re-locating in Portstewart has brought even more happiness and contentment for Billy and Lily.

"We have enjoyed being closer to our families and besides we have a lovely sea view, " says Billy who was also pleased that all the other houses and apartments in the Ocean Drive development were sold, leaving the O'Neills more time to spend in Florida and on cruises.

Everything however wasn't going according to plan however with Billy's plans for an entertainment complex due to be called the Linenhall Forum in Ballymoney and after a number of setbacks he decided to sell off most of the property he'd acquired in his home town though he did keep one shop in High Street.

22

Farewell to Sally, the Big Man and piddling in the Pope's loo

The O'Neills were deeply upset in May 2013 when Lily's mother Sally died at the age of 91. She was buried in the churchyard of Red Rock Presbyterian Church in Armagh beside her military hero husband Harry who was to feature heavily in Lily and Billy's lives some years later, gaining them national headlines. However the O'Neills were later given another reality check about the impact of one aspect of WW2 when they flew to Krakow in Poland where one of their top priorities was to visit the notorious concentration camp Auschwitz where over 1.1 million men, women and children were killed by the Nazis during the war.

Rev Dr Ian RK Paisley, Lord Bannside

Billy and Lily and Fr. Langan SJ

"We had seen so many films and read so many stories about Auschwitz that I wanted to see for myself what human people did to human people. But once I saw it I knew that I never wanted to see it again, though I will never forget that visit. I spent my 73rd birthday in Krakow but I didn't feel like celebrating. It was all too horrifying, " says Billy who signed what was known as a 'Dedication of a Peace Person' from the Peace People here which read:

"I have a simple message to the world from this movement for Peace.

I want to live and love and build a just and peaceful society.

I want for children, as I want for myself, life at home, at work, and at play to be a life of Joy and Peace. I recognise that to build such a society demands of me dedication, hard work, and courage. I recognise that there are many problems in my society which are a source of conflict and violence. I recognise that every bullet fired and every exploding bomb make that work more difficult. I reject the use of the bomb and the bullet and all the techniques of violence. I dedicate myself to working with our neighbours, near and far, day in and day out, to build that peaceful society in which the tragedies we have known are a bad memory and a continuing warningTop of Form

Bottom of FormA well-known figure in Northern Irish politics soon came onto the scene for Billy after he got a message to contact the former Stormont minister Richard Needham who'd led a number of government departments, notably holding the economic brief. But Englishman Mr Needham had another lesser-known side to his life because he was also Lord Kilmorey from County Down and he'd heard that Billy had bought some Kilmorey uniforms at an auction of items from the Kilmorey estate. At a meeting Billy reminded Mr Needham that the two men had met before at a tourism conference in the Causeway Coast Hotel in Portrush and that the politician was an MP for a part of Kent that the young O'Neill knew well from his time working on the building of the BP oil refinery on the Isle of Grain. Once the pleasantries were over Needham said he was trying to help raise the £13 million needed to refurbish the HMS Caroline warship – the only surviving vessel from the Battle of Jutland - that was permanently docked in the Titanic Quarter in Belfast. And Mr Needham whose uncle had commanded the Caroline said that he wanted to bring a couple of naval

A good friend Nigel Davidson 4th May 1961 -17 July 2021

officers over from Portsmouth to view the uniforms which included full dress and everyday uniforms with hats and great coats.

The year 2013 brought an emotional reunion for the O'Neills with Fr Langan who had not only married them in Glasgow but had also celebrated their Ruby anniversary with them.

By the July of that year the Jesuit was now in a home for retired priests in Preston and he was in a wheelchair and suffering from Parkinson's Disease. But Lily and Billy took him out for lunch and they say he was still in sparkling form and made his visitors laugh heartily. In the Italian restaurant he was asked if he had ever met the Pope and the priest said no but added: "I peed in the same loo as him!"

In the September Billy and Lily flew to Glasgow to celebrate their 52nd wedding anniversary at a Mass where the priest said Fr Langan was fondly remembered as Father Jimmy and the next month the O'Neills sent their felicitations, a card and a gift to him on his 87th birthday.

However, the next months brought more sad funerals for Billy and Lily including that of Albert Rohdich who was a friend for 47 years, Margo Evans who was their hairdresser and Uel Hammond from Burns and Hammond property services agency who had a legion of stories to tell about Ballymoney's characters.

Billy was shocked in September 2014 to hear of the death of the former Northern Ireland First Minister the Rev Ian Paisley, Lord Bannside who had led the Democratic Unionist Party and was for years the Moderator of the Free Presbyterian Church.

Shortly after his death Billy received messages on his answer machine from Baroness Eileen Paisley and from Ian Paisley junior MP to contact them.

Says Billy: " They informed me that Dr Paisley had said before his death that he wanted Lily and me to be invited to a memorial service of thanksgiving for his life and ministry on Sunday, October 19. Lily and I had a good relationship with Dr Paisley and one meeting stands out in particular. We met him at the North West 200 motorbike races one year when I had lent several caravans to the organiser Billy Nutt. When I called to see if he had enough caravans Dr Paisley was with him and the moment I opened the door he said 'that man's father made the best ice cream in Ireland.'"

The DUP had used Billy's Causeway Coast Hotel for their party conference and Billy used to say that his staff sold very little alcohol but plenty of ice-cream.

Billy recalls too that Dr Paisley arrived at Stranocum Hall one day to ask if he could rent an office for the DUP in the property that the O'Neills had bought in Ballymoney. "I accommodated him and we became friends," adds Billy "I remember when at Stranocum Hall when Lily gave the DUP leader something to eat but sadly in the middle of the meal he had to leave because a policeman had been shot."

"However he came back the following day with a bunch of flowers for Lily and he asked her if she had any more of the soup that she had given him 24 hours earlier. Which she had because she always made soup in big batches. And Dr Paisley sat down to eat two bowls of the soup and off he went, "says Billy.

Around the same time as Dr Paisley's passing, another funeral that the O'Neills attended was for the widow of a man who, like Billy, had been an influential figure in tourism on the North Coast.

Jack Fawcett had owned the Northern Counties Hotel in Portrush and Billy admired him and his wife Elsie for their determination to move on with their business during the troubles. At one point Jack approached Billy to see if he had any interest in buying his hotel but the offer was declined because he was in the process of building the Causeway Coast Hotel and Apartments at the time.

The subsequent fate of the iconic Northern Counties was not a happy one. After Jack retired and sold the hotel it was hoped the new owner would bring it back to its former glory days. But in February and March 1990 two fires gutted the hotel which had to be demolished. Billy, like thousands of other people in the area, was shattered at the loss of the 'glorious heart' of Portrush where now only memories remained.

Happily, says Billy, a new hotel currently called The Atlantic, was built on the site of the old Northern Counties. Jack Fawcett who had also owned Fawcett's Hotel beside the Northern Counties had many strings to his bow. And after his retirement when he was in his 80s he ran a class in computers for pensioners called: 'Teaching older dogs new tricks."

Jack had taken a computer course 11 years earlier and discovered that he had a gift for passing on his newly-acquired knowledge to others as a teacher. Billy O'Neill enrolled in the course and listened as Jack preached his gospel that computers couldn't be learnt about in books because there was too much 'useless' jargon inside the pages.

The late Belfast Telegraph columnist Billy Simpson who was from Portrush was intrigued by the course and wrote about it, saying that Jack had a humorous approach and believed in being on hand to help his students "There is no pressure," he told Simpson. "There are no exams.. You learn at your own speed and take out what you need from the class."

Billy says Jack got through to a 'small part of my brain', adding: "The rest was more difficult so I gave up."

But Billy and Lily never gave up their interest in dancing. And in September 2014 Billy was chuffed to be asked to use his expertise to judge a competition for charity. The event was held in the Magherabuoy Hotel which was once Jack and Elsie Fawcett's home.

But still there were funerals. In October 2014 Billy attended the funeral of Jim McMurtry who was the architect of the apartments and the Causeway Coast Hotel and Conference Centre and he was also a member of the Round Table and the 41 Club ex-Tablers

Billy and Lily had a lucky escape in April of 2015 when they went on a cruise after spending a few weeks in their Fort Myers home. The couple went on a sightseeing tour on the island of Tortola in the British Virgin Islands on a safari-style truck that ran into a major problem as it tried to go up a road on the side of a mountain. Billy says he heard a bang and realised immediately that the prop/drive shaft had snapped, sending the vehicle hurtling at speed back down the hill but the driver managed to reverse it into a sturdy crash barrier that stopped it from plunging down a 1500ft drop or smashing into another bus behind and its driver gave thanks to the Lord before ordering the O'Neills and the rest of the passengers a replacement bus. Fortunately no-one who was on the open truck tour was injured.

But there was trouble up ahead. After returning to Fort Myers a relieved Billy and Lily again indulged their passion for music by heading to New Orleans but the drive back was long and arduous with the O'Neills completing the 774 miles journey in 13 hours not including a couple of stops along the way.

Back in Florida it appeared that the marathon drive had taken its toll. Billy's left leg became sore and hard and he suspected he might have deep vein thrombosis (DVT). But he didn't seek medical attention in the States because he feared that if DVT was confirmed he wouldn't be allowed to board a plane a couple of days later to fly back to Ireland.

On his return Billy's GP advised him to go to A&E immediately and he was indeed diagnosed with DVT and prescribed a course of tablets which cleared up the condition.

Friends and relations including Sharon Chambers, Essie Jack and Jean Campbell passed away in 2015 along with a man who had been influential as Billy started to build his business in Northern Ireland. Tony O'Connor a founding partner of the commercial property firm O'Connor, Kennedy and Turtle had been the man that Billy first met 41 years earlier when he made inquiries about buying Mrs Katherine Kelly's Burnside Road caravan park and he also purchased other properties from him down the years.

A happier landmark came in December 2015 when the O'Neills' first grandchild, Arlene was married to David Pudner in Burton-on-Trent in the Cotswolds, a forerunner to the arrival nearly four years later of Billy and Lily's first great grandchild, Emily Elizabeth Grace Pudner

Ivor Boyd, Max Pollock & Dan McCook NW200 Bike fans of the world famous Joey, Robert & William Dunlop

23

Football, fast bikes and
famous faces

Billy was an enthusiastic supporter of two of the biggest sporting events on the Northern Ireland calendar. He had always enjoyed the world famous North West 200 motorcycle races which had became his busiest time of the year as a hotel owner and caravan park proprietor as Portrush, Portstewart and the surrounding towns and villages dealt with an influx of 150,000 visitors. Such was the appeal of the NW200 that fans were drawn from all over Europe and thousands of bikers descended on the North Coast including the triple Oscar winning actor Daniel Day Lewis who mingled with other enthusiasts, many of whom didn't even recognise him.

O'Neill's Caravans sales and distributors - for many years sponsors of the Northwest 200

Sponsoring Phillip McCallam

Northwest 200

Billy was also a fervent supporter of the Milk Cup football competition (later re-branded the Super Cup) which attracted hundreds of young stars of tomorrow like David Beckham, Gary Neville and Paul Scholes of Manchester United to the North Coast.

The O'Neills always tried to attend the launch ceremonies for the competition and the parades of the young hopefuls in Coleraine. A dinner in the Lodge Hotel in the town to celebrate the 25th anniversary of the tournament in 2008 was particularly enjoyable for Billy whose fondness for the Milk Cup was matched only by his admiration for one of its founders, Bertie Peacock, a man that people often told him he looked like.

And in a newspaper article to mark the 25th anniversary of the Milk Cup Billy reflected on his associations with Bertie and with the competition. The report said that while Billy was well known for his prowess on the dance floor he regretted that he hadn't stuck with his early love of football. But he said he often told Bertie that while the mercurial Celtic star used his feet to play football in his youth, Billy used his for dancing. Billy was described in the article as one of the unsung heroes of the Milk Cup for his support and for his provision of accommodation for so many visiting teams. Tournament chairman Victor Leonard described him as 'a man for all seasons' and said that while sponsors and backers had come and gone Billy had been a 'rock solid benefactor' whose backing had been greatly appreciated.

He added: "Billy isn't one to trumpet his input from the rooftops. He has always gone out of his way to help us and he has done that in a manner that has been modest and unassuming." In the same article Billy said that it had always been thrilling to see the young footballers living the dream and enjoying their experiences and getting on with each other. Billy also said it was great to see Northern Ireland getting a more positive profile around the world at a time when it was known for civil strife and loss of life.

In the article, Billy also recalled the boost he and Lily received when the Milk Cup relocated the tournament headquarters to his Causeway Coast Hotel venue where the O'Neills were able to welcome the likes of Denis Law, Pat Jennings and Graeme Souness to their complex which the newspaper article writer said became 'the place to be' during the competition.

Sir Alex Ferguson

24

The O'Neills' search for a war hero's medals

B illy and Lily found themselves firmly in the media spotlight in the summer of 2017. It came after several newspapers reported on the amazing discovery of war medals which had been won by Lily's hero father Harry. This is how the story was covered by me in a feature in the Belfast Telegraph on August 5 accompanied by a photograph taken by the legendary Coleraine photographer Mark Jamieson who tragically died in August 2018. "A Portstewart woman has finally been re-united with the five medals won by her war hero father over 70 years ago when he was commended for his

Lily's Mother Sally and Father Harry's Wedding, her Granny and Grandfather & Guests

bravery following the Normandy Landings where he was badly wounded the day after saving a colleague's life.

Sgt Harry Staddon's decorations including his prestigious Military Medal for gallantry, which, it's thought, vanished from the soldier's home in Portrush in the 1970s, were found after Lily O'Neill's family conducted an exhaustive search which stretched all the way from Ireland, England and Wales to Australia and back again.

But Mrs O'Neill also received an added bonus – a citation in recognition of Harry Staddon's bravery, signed by Field Marshal Bernard Montgomery himself.

Monty wrote how Harry courageously organised the men in his platoon in response to heavy fire from German positions in August 1944, two months after the 2nd Monmouthshire Regiment landed in Normandy as part of the 53rd Welsh Division.

The British Commander-in-Chief said Harry's quick thinking led to a 25 strong German platoon surrendering.

But shortly afterwards Harry was back in action, selflessly rushing to the aid of one of his men who had been hit by shellfire which ignited a grenade and set him on fire.

"This NCO stripped off the man's clothing and equipment and extinguished the phosphorus which was burning," said Monty who added that Harry set an example 'which could not be improved upon.'

The citation continued: "On the following day during the attack on Leffard whilst leading and encouraging his men he was wounded."

Doctors carried out no fewer than 22 operations on injuries to Harry's leg but they couldn't save it.

After two years in hospital in England, the London-born soldier returned to Northern Ireland where he'd been stationed.

He'd met his wife Sally in Newry and they set up home in Armagh where he worked as a boiler man before moving to a similar job in Coleraine hospital.

He and his family lived in Hopefield Avenue in Portrush where Harry who had an artificial leg kept his medals in a drawer. But he eventually discovered that his medals were missing and it was impossible to establish where they'd gone. Harry died on October 19, 1985 at the age of 67 without ever finding out what happened to his precious medals.

But his daughter Lily and her husband Billy O'Neill never gave up hope, though they accepted that the chances of recovering the medals were slim.

However one evening, a couple of years ago, as they watched TV coverage of Remembrance Day commemorations in London with their grandson David, the first steps were taken in the hunt for the medals, with a little help from technology.

Lily said: "I happened to mention to David that his great-grandfather had fought in the war but all his medals went missing from the house in Portrush."

Lily with father's medals

David went onto Google on his smartphone and within minutes he found records showing that Harry's medals had been bought and sold by a series of collectors down the years.

"They'd been all around the world," said Lily. "There was documentation to prove they had been in the hands of private collectors in Australia and England."

Lily's husband Billy wasn't prepared to stop there, however and he set about tracing the latest owners of the medals.

He telephoned and emailed a number of dealers who'd been involved in the earlier transactions but they were reluctant to share information with him.

However then came a stroke of luck as Billy learnt by chance from a relative across the water that Harry's medals were back on the market with a dealer in Wales.

Said Billy: "I contacted him but I didn't say who I was and I made an offer which was accepted."

After the medals were safely back in Northern Ireland, Billy revealed his identity to the dealer who told him that the price would have been higher if he'd known he was a member of Harry's family.

"I said that was why I hadn't told him," laughed Billy.

Lily said she was overjoyed to have the medals returned to her family along with the Field Marshal Montgomery citation which she'd never seen before.

"That was very special to see," she added."We had copies of the medals but they're not the same as the real things"

Lily said her father was a modest man. "He never talked about the war. He'd been a very fit and strong man who'd been a weightlifter and a PT instructor. He also trained boxers in his day."

Billy said: "Harry was a very quiet man but the citation shows just how brave he was in the heat of battle in France."

Harry's son-in-law is still keen to put all the missing pieces of the medals' jigsaw together.

"I want to trace their journey but I'd also like to know how the medals disappeared in the first place," he said.

The Montgomery citation has a special place in Lily and Billy's home.

It reads in full: "On 14 Aug 44 at about 2100 hours this NCO (Harry Staddon) was leading his platoon in the area X rds 041407 when he came under fire from a German locality to the East. He organised a fire plan quickly and chiefly due to quick resolution the German platoon surrendered and about 25 prisoners were captured. Shortly afterwards in the same area when a man was hit by shell fire and his 77 grenade was ignited this NCO stripped off the man's clothing and equipment and extinguished the phosphorous which was burning him.Throughout this period this NCO set an example which could not be improved upon. On the following day during the attack on Leffard, map ref 0638 whilst leading and

Lily and Billy

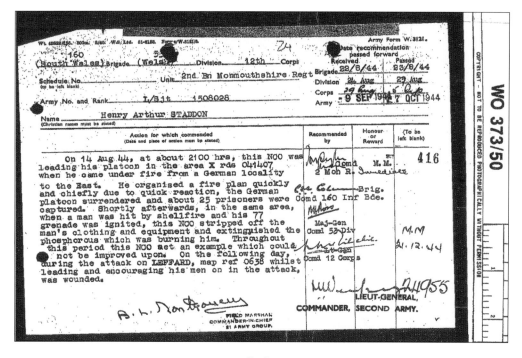

Citation

encouraging his men on in this attack he was wounded. "Signed, Montgomery, Field Marshal, Commander-in-Chief, 21 Army Group.

The O'Neills joy over the return of Harry Staddon's medals was tempered in September 2017 by the death of Billy's sister-in-law Joan who passed away in Rochester in Kent. Billy had lived with Joan and his brother Hughie from 1956 to 1960 and her death hit him hard.

Billy and Lily travelled to England in October for Joan's funeral with her son Loren, his wife Lin and their children Tara and Kieran, joining her other son Dean and his family for the service.

"We also visited a memorial tree for Hughie in the same grounds and then we celebrated Joan's life in the Robin Hood pub in Chatham, Kent," says Billy.

The O'Neills' quest in regard to Lily's father and his war service wasn't over. Far from it. And in June 2019 they joined a coach tour of the sites of the Normandy Landings organised by the chairman of Ballymoney Royal British Legion, Mark McLaughlin.

It was a long and arduous three day journey by road and ferries from Larne to Cairnryan and from Poole in Dorset to Cherbourg with two overnight stops on the way.

The papers were again full of the O'Neills' story.

The Coleraine Chronicle report started:

"Portstewart woman Lily O'Neill recently joined many from across the world who travelled to the Normandy beaches 75 years after the famous allied landings, laying a wreath where her father won the Military Medal for bravery.

Lily described the moment as "very emotional" remembering not only her beloved father, Lance Corporal Henry 'Harry' Staddon, but the other men who fought in some of the fiercest fighting of WW2.

Readers may remember two years ago in August 2017, The Chronicle reported the amazing story of how Harry's war medals were recovered by Lily's husband, Ballymoney man Billy O'Neill, MBE.

The medals had been missing for many years until a chance remark among family members led to a search, with Billy tracking down the precious heirlooms in Wales and buying them back.

Now Billy, who again took the lead, moving things along on another poignant step, said: "When I was informed that Ballymoney Royal British Legion were organising a trip to Normandy on June 7 and Rotarians were welcome I immediately booked two seats for Lily and me and it was a real experience."

Speaking at her Portstewart home, Lily took up the story, saying: "I laid a wreath at the monument on Hill 112 remembering the divisions who fought there including the 53rd Welsh Division that my dad fought with."

The monument had been unveiled in 2015 by Prince Edward. Lily said the visit and the laying of the wreath had been 'very emotional' adding: "I get upset just thinking about it, not just for my father but for all the men, it's awfully sad."

The weather wasn't good but Lily said she was glad that she and Billy had gone to Normandy because they got a lot from the trip and from the visit to a German cemetery which 'was just as sad.'

Officials from the Ballymoney RBL had found the village of Laffard where Lily's dad was injured.

Mark McLaughlin said it was hugely satisfying to take Lily to the area where her father earned his Military Medal because it epitomised everything the Legion was all about – remembrance.

Looking back Billy says the week-long trip allowed coach guests to see a lot of well-known wartime locations.

"We visited an area known as Point du Hoc where we saw the remains of the heavily defended cliff tops occupied by the Germans. And driving along the coast we passed Omaha Beach and went to the village of Arromanches where we saw what remains of the Mulberry Harbours deployed by the Allies on the beaches. That was on day four of the tour and the next day we visited Pegasus Bridge, Coleville Montgomery (where there's a statue of Field Marshal Montgomery) and Sword Beach where the 2nd Battalion Royal Ulster Rifles went ashore during Operation Overlord which was the codename for the Allied invasion of Normandy. On day six we went to the town of Bayeux, famous for its Cathedral and medieval tapestry before going to an American cemetery near the village of St Laurent.

The journey home was on the Cherbourg to Rosslare ferry and back home on the coach. It was a superbly organised tour by the Royal British Legion who couldn't have done anything more to make it extra special for Lily."

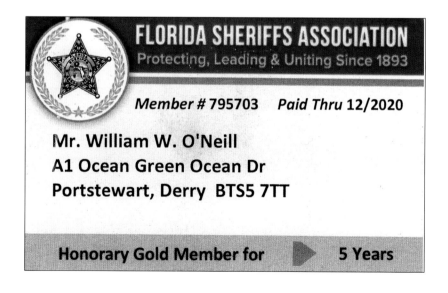

25

In mourning for more relations and good friends

B illy's who'd had operations to remove cataracts was also suffering from a painful knee which was playing up and an X ray showed he would eventually need a new one. But his issues were put into perspective by the passing of more friends including former Metropolitan Police Officer Jim Bannon, the son of an RUC man from Union Street in Ballymoney and of Barney Fitzpatrick, a Past President of the Rotary Club in Ballymoney. From West Belfast Barney had also been a well-known member of the RUC and PSNI for 40 years reaching the rank of Chief Superintendent and receiving the Queen's Police Medal for services to the public.

Late William Dunlop

Billy says that after his retirement Barney, who was wounded in the course of his policing duties, joined the Alliance Party in 2006 and served on Coleraine Borough Council where he worked tirelessly for reconciliation. "He was also the life and soul of the party, "says Billy. "He had a wealth of jokes and yarns to tell."

Former neighbours from the Rodden Foot also passed away including Ann McCotter and Francie Mills who had once sent Billy a treasured picture of residents from the area on Victory in Europe day (May 8 1945). Billy and his mother were both in the photograph.

Lily's only brother Dennis died of a heart attack on his way to work in June 2018 and it was a dreadful shock for the O'Neills for whom he had worked with for many years as a driver and an installer of caravans on the parks.

Historian Alex Blair, the secretary of Ballymoney's acclaimed amateur drama festival which was supported by O'Neills' caravans and who gave talks on Stranocum Hall and its history died soon afterwards.

But on July 18 came the shock death of a young man whose tragic passing touched the O'Neills and thousands of people in Northern Ireland, in Britain and around the world.

For William Dunlop was a motor cycle rider whose supreme skills earned him victory after victory and followed the tradition of his famous family. William was the latest member of the Dunlop dynasty to perish doing what he loved doing – racing. His father Robert was another legend on two wheels who died in a crash on the North West 200 circuit in May 2008.

William was also a nephew of one of the sport's most idolised riders, Joey Dunlop who died during a race in Estonia in July 2000. Billy attended all three funerals which were among the biggest ever witnessed in Northern Ireland with thousands of people showing their respects including hundreds of motorcycle fans from right across the globe.

Every year thousands of bikers visit the memorial gardens built in Ballymoney to honour the Dunlops in Castle Street in Ballymoney where Billy's grandparents Hugh and Lizzie Ramsey ran a shop until they moved to Armoy.

Also in July Lily and Billy attended the funeral service for renowned press photographer Mark Jamieson – and a dear friend of the author of this book - who died, aged just 60 after a short illness.

Billy and Lily's 57th wedding anniversary on September 23, 2018 brought a brief respite from the sad times with the return to an old haunt, Coleraine's Boat House on the banks of the River Bann which had become home to the Water Margin Chinese restaurant.

In its former guise, the Boat House was the venue for dances in the 1950s when the resident band were The Woodchoppers. But less than a month after the O'Neills' wedding celebrations Billy received the devastating news that his niece Bernadette had died in Spain at the age of 61.

Billy didn't believe in doing things by half or doing them purely for himself. So after an intimate dinner for his actual 80th birthday in Coleraine's Water Margin restaurant on November 23, 2019 he pushed the boat out for a bigger, grander celebration to help raise money for charity a week later. One hundred and sixty guests were invited to the party in the Royal Court Hotel in Portrush on November 30 2019.

Son Terry set up a presentation on a big screen with a gallery of pictures including ones from Buckingham Palace in 2007 when the Queen gave his father his MBE.

A full colour brochure was also produced with a caricature of Billy on the front cover drawn by artist Goldie along with a headline that said he was '80 years young' comparing him to a wine, a vintage 1939 with a distinctive, robust and full of character. Inside were pictures of Billy and Lily down the years, some of them in their distinctive dancing gear and others with their ever-expanding family.

The menu was also presented in full along with the running order of the night's proceedings.

The entertainment came from Fiddler Adam and Plug and Dominic and guests donated £6,105 for Ballymoney Rotary Club's charities. The only downside was Billy's sister Jean was unable to attend the soiree because of ill-health.

It was on a Friday the 13th (of December 2019) that Billy and Lily received more news that they had been dreading – with the death of their friend, Fr Langan SJ, who had played such an influential part in their young lives after they eloped to Glasgow.

The phone call from St Wilfrid's Church in Preston with the news devastated the O'Neills. They had kept in touch with the priest ever since he married them in Scotland and they always told him they couldn't thank him enough for what he had done for them in Glasgow. Even as his health was declining Billy and Lily were always keen to see him and to help. On his 90th birthday a few years before his passing they had gone over to Preston to visit him. They took him out for dinner but they were conscious that his Parkinson's disease was hitting him hard.

Billy says: "Although he was able to watch TV in a lounge with other retired priests it was more difficult for him to move about. He had a large bedroom and we wanted to buy him a TV for his birthday for his room but he refused to have one. He spent a lot of time in prayer and reading but with the Parkinson's he was finding it difficult to write and his voice was getting weaker and harder to understand.

"Fr. Jimmy, as he liked to be called, was born in the same year as the Queen and he was one of the most Christian people I have ever met. I still find it nearly impossible to find the words to describe his goodness, kindness, friendliness and his generosity to those in need no matter about their creed, colour, or background. He never criticised and he had a wonderful sense of humour and such a joyful laugh."

Billy and Lily were unable to attend the funeral of the man they dubbed their 'angel' because they were flying out to America for four months. However their son Terry attended the funeral on their behalf and Stephen and his wife Sandra offered their sympathy.

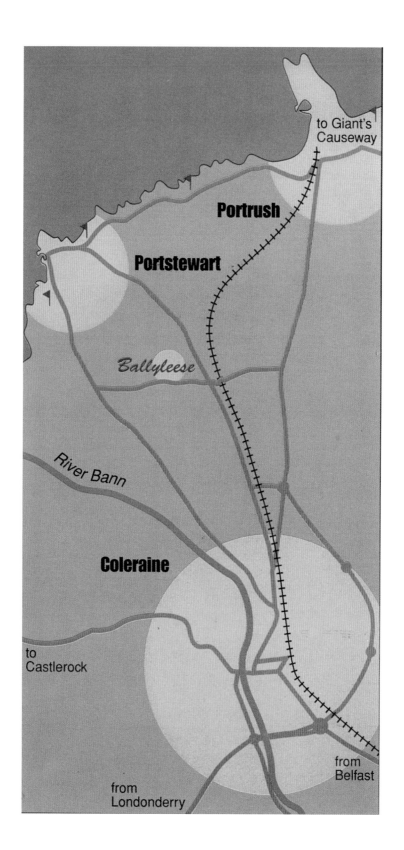

to Giant's
Causeway

Portrush

Portstewart

Ballyleese

River Bann

Coleraine

to
Castlerock

from
Belfast

from
Londonderry

171

In Fort Myers the O'Neills encountered problems with their holiday home which had needed repairs to the roof but they weren't carried out leaving Billy and Lily feeling let down by the contractors.

After returning from a Caribbean cruise on the Celebrity Silhouette Billy and Lily were still unhappy with the lack of repairs at Fort Myers but there were other shocks in store.

They discovered that an American couple whom they had met through friends and who had stayed with the O'Neills at Stranocum Hall after their wedding, had been living in the Florida house without the permission of Billy and Lily - whose suspicions had been raised by the size of the bills they were receiving for their Fort Myers property.

Billy rang the unauthorised 'guest' who immediately said sorry and offered to pay the rent but the apology didn't wash and he and his wife were asked to leave.

The concerns over the repairs and the increasing difficulties with the house – another group of people had also used the house without permission – made up Billy and Lily's minds that they should put the property on the market.

The sale wasn't easy but eventually the O'Neills received an offer matching the asking price and they agreed to sell the house. . "We had no regrets in the end," says Billy who while he was in America started hearing a new worrying word – Coronavirus - on the news bulletins. And like millions of people around the world he and Lily became more and more concerned about COVID-19 as the Coronavirus continued to tighten its grip globally.

Terry phoned them in America and told them that if they didn't come home immediately they might not get back at all because the pandemic was shutting down airports at an alarming rate.

Terry managed to bring his parents' flights forward and in a hurry they packed as many of their personal items as they could into their luggage which included two hastily purchased new suitcases.

As they departed they instructed their estate agent Gary Young to sell the Fort Myers house with all its furniture, excluding paintings of the north coast back home and their beloved Arcadia ballroom in Portrush.

"We lost four weeks of our holiday in the States," adds Billy: "But our health is our wealth"

Safely back in Northern Ireland, Billy says he and Lily adhered strictly to the COVID regulations during the Government-ordered lockdown and 'better still' barely had a drink.

"We felt all the better for it, "says Billy. "But we never went to a pub to get drunk anyway. Drinking for us was a couple of glasses of wine with a meal, at a dance or the theatre. We owned the Kosey Korner bar in Ballymoney and we never had a drink in it!"

Just after the pandemic started to really have an impact, another caravan park was added to the O'Neill family portfolio. Terry's friends David and Olive Dunlop who had bought Pemberton caravans from him over the years let it be known they wanted to sell their caravan park in Bushmills called Ballyness. Terry's son Conor bought the park and now carries on the family business.

It was a baptism of fire, said the Belfast Telegraph in an article about the difficulties that Coronavirus had caused to caravan park owners and the people who caravanned in them. Terry talked to the newspaper about the crisis facing the industry saying: "We rely heavily on caravan sales and we haven't sold a caravan since lockdown. I've been speaking to other park operators in the area and everybody is struggling at the moment to keep their business afloat because the pitch fee is heavily subsidised through caravan sales." Terry also spoke to the Telegraph about his son Conors difficult start at Ballyness. He said: "We had one weekend and then we just had to close up during the lockdown. First we closed the public buildings and then we saw it wasn't getting any better and we pulled the plug on the whole thing. It's certainly been a tough start to a new business venture," he says. "The response by the Government has been helpful and reassuring but I'm also worried about the future." Conor said they lost 60% of their touring caravan business when they had to be cancelled. He issued refunds to the tune of around £40,000, but thankfully was back up and running in July. It was a tough start to the new business venture in 2020 but all our customers have been very understanding about it being a bad time for everybody."

Four people continued to use their holiday homes on the Parks during lockdown with the approval of the PSNI because they were unable to live at home due to the rules surrounding self-isolation. Another couple were self-isolating at the caravan park because their daughter was a student nurse living at the family home while she working on the frontline coping with the pandemic. Conor told the Telegraph "We're allowed to operate within a very tight window, it's not for holiday use. It's important people still obey the restrictions." The paper said Conor believed the caravan sector would be a safer option for people to go to on breaks once the restrictions began to relax a little. "I'm optimistic that we will see things opening up a little in August or maybe even the end of July, hopefully," he said. "We can operate safely. Our caravans are all 10 metres apart and they're self-contained. They're like miniature service apartments. I feel that we could operate safely at half capacity. But it's the travelling around that the Government wants to stop."

Billy and Lily made themselves available in any way they could with the caravans to help their offspring who during lockdown installed PPE, screens, specialised cleaning products, COVID-19 signage and hand sanitisers. The restrictions on movement during the lockdown however meant that it wasn't until August when the rules were relaxed a little that Billy and Lily could meet their great granddaughter Emily Elizabeth Grace for the first time with her parents Arlene and David. "The same month Leanne our step-granddaughter and her husband Chris McGrath had a baby boy, Harris Alexander McGrath." says Billy who was able to re-pay an unusual debt in January 2021 despite the pandemic.

Because of the COVID-19 regulations there was no formal 90th birthday party for Billy's brother David who had given him a watch in 1956 to sell to raise the money to pay for his travel to England. "I thought it was high time that I presented David with a new watch and there was no time like his 90th birthday to thank him for what he did and for being the cement which holds our family together," says Billy who a month later was attending 'my saddest ever funeral.' Owen McMullan (25) and Brigid Wilkinson (21) were killed in a two vehicle collision near Ballycastle in February 2021 leaving three very young children orphans. "Owen was the son of my niece Ann who worked with us in our shop at Ballyreagh and at our holiday park in Portstewart. Seeing Owen and Brigid being buried together was heart-breaking," says Billy who lost his brother Dessie to lung cancer the following month and in April the O'Neills sent a sympathy card to the Queen after the death of Prince Philip, the Duke of Edinburgh. The Queen responded with a card that read: "I send you my sincere thanks for your kind words of sympathy on the death of my husband. Elizabeth R."

Billy says he spent some emotional times with his ailing sister Jean who'd been unable to go to his 60th anniversary celebrations. "We reminisced about our family and about the Rodden Foot," says Billy. And there were more journeys down memory lane in July when Billy called to see another caravan business owner Tom Blair and his wife Ethel. Says Billy: "We talked about our early days in the caravan business and how it has changed from the 50's and 60's, from the old buses and railway carriages converted to holidays homes at Ballyreagh, to the modern holiday parks with full amenity pitches; to manufactured holiday homes with under-floor insulation, double glazing, central heating, piped gas, TV and smart phones, making holidaying at home a real joy."

In July 2021 within a 48 hour period Billy heard about the passing of two friends – Frank Campbell who serviced the clocks in Stranocum Hall and Nigel Davidson, a business consultant who had helped him enormously over the years passed away the day after preparing food parcels at his Jordan Victory Church in Carrickfergus.

The pandemic restrictions were still playing havoc with normal life for everyone around the world but in August Lily and Billy were able to attend a reunion concert in Kelly's Village, Portrush for one of their favourite bands Clubsound who had been a massively popular draw for years in Northern Ireland, especially at the Causeway Coast Hotel, with their own brand of comedy and song."They still sounded just the same," says Billy. "We had a good night's entertainment and we also had a wee dance."

Billy's Sister Elizabeth

26

Six decades of marriage celebrated

The O'Neills didn't allow the Coronavirus to totally disrupt their plans to celebrate their 60th wedding anniversary in the Royal Court Hotel overlooking the stunning White Rocks beach in Portrush on September 23,2021. It was also the third wedding anniversary of the O'Neills step-daughter Leanne and her husband Chris McGrath., But because of COVID-19 it was decided to limit the guest list to just 33 family members and close friends.

On the morning of the anniversary Billy and Lily were thrilled to discover that one of the messages of congratulations had come from the Queen.

Family photo at Billy and Lily's 60th Diamond Anniversary Royal Court Hotel Portrush

At the Royal Court the menu was a flashback in time. For the starter of melon or soup followed by a main course of roast beef and a dessert of pavalova was exactly the same menu as Fr Langan had organised for Billy and Lily in the Grand Central Hotel in Glasgow on their wedding day.

Their friend Alice Rohdich had baked a special cake designed by Billy as a 'nod' to their elopement. It showed Lily's family home at Islay View in Bushmills with a ladder at the window and a motorbike outside. It also had a representation of a £45 18 ft Bluebird caravan on top.

On a night the O'Neills would never forget Billy delivered a passionate speech reflecting on the happiness of the couple's marriage and thanking Lily for her love.

Billy started his address by saying: "Family, friends and my diamond wife Lily of 60 years. Welcome to tonight's celebration of this miracle – I mean marriage - of 60 years between Lily and I. In March 1960 I returned from England after the contract ended where I worked as a trainee diesel mechanic for Sir Robert McAlpine. I lived with my brother Hughie and his wife Joan for four years. I obtained a job in the Braid Water spinning mill on night shift and I bought a 250cc BSA motor bike for transport. The 19th of May 1960 was a date I will always remember. Four things happened for me that day, first I passed my test on my motorbike; second I met my future wife Lily Staddon in the Arcadia ballroom; third it was the first time I was ever inside a caravan and caravans became our family business; fourth was to meet my future mother-in-law Mrs Sally Staddon. I became her favourite son-in-law because I was the only one.

"Lily and I married each other three times(renewing our vows twice). Once Kaelan said to us: "Nanny Lily and granddad Billy why did you marry three times when all you do is argue!?" Lily said it was to be sure, to be sure, to be sure. I said the only good thing about marrying the same woman three times is that you only have one mother-in-law.

"Len Goodman from Strictly when he interviewed me asked what I thought when I first saw Lily. I said she was like a puppet on a string, out of control but was very good at dancing backwards in high heels which he had to think about. Lily and I loved dancing, then we fell in love. We were inseparable until I broke my leg on August 26, 1960 on my motorbike. I was on the way for a job interview in the townland of Billy as I was made redundant at Fison's. When the ambulance driver arrived he said "I know you, you will not be dancing with Harry Staddon's daughter for a while." I said "I have a date with Lily at 3 pm at the entrance to Ratheane hospital where she works." The ambulance happened to arrive at Ratheane Hospital at dead on 3 pm. The driver stopped and said to Lily "I have someone here who knows you," and I said to her "even with a broken leg I kept my date."

Billy re-visited many other significant milestones that he has talked about in this book, the death of his mother; the warning from Mrs Staddon to stop seeing her daughter because of their differing religions; the eloping to Scotland; the kindness of Fr Langan; the couple's love of dancing; the moves to work in England; the return to Northern Ireland, the building of a caravan business and the Causeway Coast Hotel and Apartments. Billy told his guests that he and Lily had seen small and large weddings at their restaurant and hotel including one with no fewer than 250 guests and three cakes!

"When I look back our wedding was as romantic as any. And here we are 60 years later," said Billy who recalled the titles he had acquired many years earlier but which the couple had, until then, never used.

He added: "So tonight I present Dame Elizabeth Grace (Lily) O'Neill, Knight Commander of the Plantagenet Toxophilites with the award of a gold medal for putting up with me for the last 60 years."

Billy also asked guests to be upstanding for a toast to absent friends including his nephew Gary who sadly died from lung cancer a short time later. Billy had requested that no-one should give him and Lily presents at their celebration but 'Terry and Stephen didn't listen.'

However the O'Neills got the chance to mark the anniversary in a very special way.

On the eve of the anniversary Billy took Lily to see a memorial garden at the Church of Ireland in Ballymoney that he had visited a short time earlier on behalf of the town's Rotary Club.

The garden and its orchard were only a few fields away from Billy's home at the Rodden Foot but he had not been aware that they were there.

By chance the minister the Rev Andrew Sweeney arrived to cut the grass and Billy asked him if he could sponsor something as a tribute to the 'many happy hours I spent in the Rodden Foot.'

It was agreed that a plaque could be put up next to the flower beds. It reads:

"In Memory of the O'Neill Family's Happy Days in the Rodden Foot Community

Lily and Billy O'Neill MBE 23rd September 2021"

Painting by our Grandson Kaelan

Lily and Billy with family and friends at 60th Diamond Wedding Anniversary

Billy' and Lily's 40th Ruby Wedding Anniversary Stranocum Hall 2001

Cutting the cake and Telegram from the Queen

27

Big hearts and big donations

Charity they say begins at home. For Billy and Lily O'Neill it's a passion that has never known any bounds, only bonds with their local community. For ever since they found that good fortune was smiling on them and their business endeavours Billy and Lily say they have been determined to share their largesse with others. It's only a rough estimate but it appears that the figure the O'Neills have given away or have helped to amass for charities and other good causes by hosting fund-raising events stands at nearly a quarter of a million pounds.

Ask the O'Neills why they are so big-hearted and chances are that they will just change the subject. But friends say that in private Billy and Lily feels a sense of satisfaction that they have been able to come to the aid of people less fortunate than themselves.

Richard Dixon, Billy, Niall, Ryan Lily and David with other fundraisers

And their generosity stretched to people and charities right across the divide in Northern Ireland.

As of June 2022 the list of charities that the O'Neills have helped to sponsor over 50 years in business included:

Stranocum and District Community Association; the Milk Cup football tournament; Rotary Club of Ballymoney, Lion's Club of Coleraine; Prince' Trust;
NI Territorial Army Field Hospital and Somme Hospital.
Ballymoney Round Table
Ballymoney Masonic Diabetes Awareness charity
Ballymoney MS
Ballymoney Drama Festival
Ballymoney- Dalriada School
Ballymoney, Special Olympics.

Armoy Motorcycle Club (barbecue)
Cullybackey Classic Vehicle Club (barbecue)

N I Charolais Cattle Club Maghera; Cancer charities; NSPCC;RNLI; Ulster Youth Orchestra; Royal British Legion; Autism charities; NI Hospice, NI Scouts; Ballymoney museum; Robert Quigg VC statue appeal

 Other charities and sporting events that the O'Neills sponsored included the North West 200 motorcycle races; a Black Bush golf competition; the NI Super Cup; the Police D.P.O.A. and RNLI raft races; RUC reconciliation events; fishing competitions; band tournaments; snooker championships; the Prince's Volunteer Trust; Action Mental Health; the BBC sports awards (2004); the Sammy Wilson Bikers Club; the Florida Sheriff's youth camps; the Rotary Club breakfast, the Rotary Club Wheelchair Foundation and latterly a charity helping the people of Ukraine.

The O'Neills' charitable efforts have been recognised with a number of awards and even a letter from Prince Charles. He wrote to thank Billy and Lily for the work they had done for the Prince's Trust and praising them for the 'warm reception' that members of the charity had received when they held a conference in the Causeway Coast Hotel. A citation from the Trust itself also 'gratefully acknowledged' the contribution saying: "Our aim is to find ways of helping the young people of our country to develop their latent talents and abilities, particularly those who might feel alienated or at a disadvantage, and thus to bolster their self-confidence which is so important for meeting life's challenges."

Other awards that came the way of the O'Neills were the 1985 British Airways Tourism Endeavour Award; a Coleraine Borough Council Volunteers' Award in 2001 for commitment and contribution; and in 2005 a 30 year membership award from the National Caravan Council, plus, of course, the MBE from the Queen in 2007.

Another award that touched Billy was what's known as a Melvin Jones Fellowship from the Lion Clubs International Foundation (LCIF).

A citation from the LCIF's chairman J Frank Moore the third in Illinois said the fellowship was in honour of its founder Melvin Jones and was the highest form of recognition conferred by the Foundation. It added in a personal message to Billy: "It is largely due to the growth of the fellowship programme that the LCIF that has been able to meet humanitarian needs in communities worldwide. As a Melvin Jones fellow your name has been added to our listing of all individuals in the programme. These names are electronically shown in continuous rotation in the LCIF recognition room at international headquarters. The exhibit stands as a tribute to a growing network of individuals who are committed to the humanitarian objectives of the LCIF. I urge you to wear your Melvin Jones fellow lapel pin with pride. It represents your dedication to making the world a better place through your humanitarian service."

Something else which made Billy proud was his drive to help to strengthen an historical link between his hometown of Ballymoney and a former President of the United States, William McKinley.

He was the 25th President of America who served from 1897 until he was assassinated by a lone gunman in Buffalo, New York in 1901 His great, great, grandfather, James McKinley, emigrated from the townland of Conagher, near Dervock, in 1743. On a trip to Billy's holiday home in Florida he got a tip-off from his friend Mark Fleming that an auction in the town of Cape Coral could hold a few hidden gems linked to McKinley. Billy duly went to the auction in a condominium just 10 miles from Fort Myers and he says: "I was amazed at the amount of McKinley memorabilia that was hanging on the walls, together with items associated with the Rotary Clubs movement. Straight away I thought Ballymoney museum could do with the material as well as the Rotary Club of Ballymoney." In the end Billy bought a plate marking the President's first speech as a senator and another one commemorating his funeral along with an armband worn during the ceremony; a President McKinley dollar and several other artefacts including campaign badges and plaques which Billy donated to grateful officials at Ballymoney Museum.

Keith Beattie who was the manager of the Museum told the Coleraine Chronicle: "We are delighted that Billy has donated this material; it is of obvious historical importance to Ballymoney. It was a source of great pride and a cause for celebration in the district when McKinley was elected."

Soon after Billy's presentation the old Dalriada room in the museum was re-named the McKinley room in honour of the President. Billy says he has always supported the Ballymoney museum which is located in the Town Hall and which promises to help visitors discover the 'vibrant history and beauty and mystery' of the town. A permanent exhibition includes the story of the area since early times including the mystical Derrykeighan Stone from which the museum takes its logo. The museum also reflects on the 1798 rebellion by the united Irishmen and its links to the Hutchinson family from Stranocum Hall. And it also has displays about Ballymoney's involvement with the two World Wars as well as the old Corfield camera factory which re-located to the town from Wolverhampton and was regarded as one of the world's leading manufacturers of 35mm cameras. The factory which closed in 1971 was once featured by Gloria Hunniford in her Travelling Picture TV show

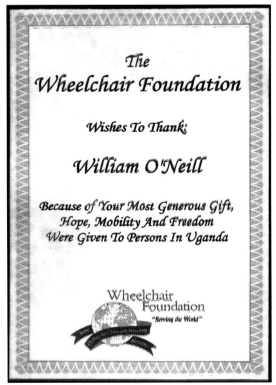

The
Wheelchair Foundation

Wishes To Thank:

William O'Neill

*Because of Your Most Generous Gift,
Hope, Mobility And Freedom
Were Given To Persons In Uganda*

Wheelchair
Foundation
"Serving the World"

Coleraine Lions Club -raise funds to buy charity holiday home

The Mayor of Coleraine, William King, opening specially designed caravan for spina bifida and hydrocephalus unit

The rotary club of Ballymoney on a visit to Loughgilphead

Billy elected as President of Coleraine Lions Club

Rotary Club of Ballymoney, Dragon Boat race

Friends Frank Campbell and Jean, Teresa Fitzpatrick with Niki and Sam Moore OBE

from Ballymoney. Billy is also pleased that the museum also, unsurprisingly, focuses heavily on the area's contribution to the history of road racing in Ireland, particularly the glory days of the Dunlop family, Joey, Robert and William.

Also remembered in the museum are two giants of the arts world who were born in Ballymoney – playwright George Shiels and the comedian James Young. Shiels (1881-1949) who was born in Ballybrakes wrote a large number of Ulster plays which were enormously popular with audiences in theatres all over Ireland including at the Abbey in Dublin during the playwright's lifetime and for years after his death.

Young (1918-1974) who was born in Ballymoney's Union Street developed his own hilarious one-man show which he performed in front of sold-out audiences in Belfast's Group Theatre and he later starred in his own television shows for the BBC, closing the ones at the start of the troubles with a plea to people to 'stop fighting.'

Other organisations to which Billy belonged through the years included The Northern Ireland Hotels Federation and Hospitality Association; Stranocum & District Community Association; The Causeway Museum Services Advisory Forum; Coleraine Round Table; Coleraine Ex-Round Tablers 41 Club; Coleraine Lions Club; Ballymoney Rotary Club; The Florida Sheriffs' Association and the Cast Iron Seat Society.

THE PRINCE'S TRUST

gratefully acknowledges
the contribution and support of

BILLY O'NEILL

"Our aim is to find ways of helping
the young people of our country to develop
their latent talents and abilities, particularly
those who might feel alienated or
at a disadvantage, and thus to bolster
their self-confidence which is so important
for meeting life's challenges"

HRH The Prince of Wales

28

The holidays

Billy worked hard and along with his ever supportive wife Lily he played hard too. And as they scaled back on their gruelling business schedules they decided to take more time to enjoy 'quality' time on holidays around the world, with cruises a particular favourite. Billy says: "We were fortunate to have two sons Terry and Stephen and their families running the caravan parks, and letting us travel when we felt like it. Sometimes one or the other family members came with us to make sure we behaved"

To list all the O'Neills' holidays and travels would require a book all on its own. But some of the highlights were as follows:

Lily and Billy meeting the Captain on their first Cruise

MAJORCA. The first holiday abroad was near Arenal in Majorca in October 1971. Billy particularly enjoyed the Spanish music in their hotel, the Tropical for the dancing.

TENERIFE First trips there were with Lily's parents. Downside was a German woman shouting 'Englander' at Harry after hearing his Cockney accent and pointing to her husband in a wheelchair as if to suggest he was in some way responsible. Harry let her see that he had lost a leg in the war and other guests cheered and applauded.

(Harry passed away in October 1985 and he was given a military send-off by the Royal British Legion) Fifteen holidays were spent in Tenerife. On another one Billy had his wallet stolen in Playa des Americas.

The thief maxed out his debit card, not once but twice before Billy could cancel it.

GRAN CANARIA. The O'Neills took Lily's widowed mother Sally to the island and were accompanied by other relatives. At the Sioux City country and western BBQ a young man got more than he bargained for when he pulled at Lily's bra strap. For she knocked him out. The next day Lily saw him on a shark fishing boat trip. He and his friends moved away.

BENALMADENA, SPAIN. Visit to Gibraltar and North Africa. Scary trip to a casbah and to the Sultan's Palace restaurant where Lily and Billy had to buy their toilet roll.

CORK, IRELAND. Visit to the Guinness Jazz Festival with friends Lily and Albert Rohdich. Went to a concert by George Melly accompanied by virtuoso fiddle player Stephane Grappelli but more to the O'Neills' taste was a show by Acker Bilk.

GERMANY. Week's boat trip on the River Rhine.

EUROPE. Tour in an American RV (recreational vehicle) called Georgie Boy. Visited Belgium Holland, Germany, France, Switzerland, Monte Carlo and Spain. Came home with 600 bottles of wine mainly for charity functions at Stranocum Hall. Later bought another 300 bottles in France.

TORREVIEJA, SPAIN. Negotiations to buy a house broke down. The house was later demolished because the builder didn't have planning permission.

FLORIDA. Bought a house in Fort Myers. Finished furnishing it during a visit in January 2004.

PARIS. Visit it to the famous sights, the Louvre and the Mona Lisa; the Eiffel Tower and Notre Dame. But Lily's purse was stolen by a pickpocket on the Champs Elysees.

NEW ORLEANS. Another favourite destination especially for the jazz on Bourbon Street and the French cuisine in restaurants like Brennan's where Lily and Billy almost got a free dinner because staff thought they were part of a visiting Irish delegation that included the Taoiseach. However the O'Neills later told the staff that they were on their own and that Billy was not Ireland's Prime Minister.

MIAMI. Just as there were highs, there were also lows for the O'Neills on their breakaways and they didn't get any worse than the night they spent in a motel near Key West, the only accommodation they could find. The TV and air conditioning unit were on a chair; there were no curtains on the windows and in the bathroom there was only one towel, one drinking glass and no hot water or shampoo or soaps. On returning from driving to a restaurant Billy and Lily were ordered to pay $15 dollars to park their car. Outside the motel cockerels and hens were running loose in scenes reminiscent of the Rodden Foot in the 50s. Another 'attraction' was an old man with a board offering to tell dirty jokes in return for a dollar bill. "I gave him a dollar but declined to hear any of his jokes," says Billy.

However insult was added to injury for Billy after he and Lily were awakened from their sleep in the middle of the night by shouting and screaming from other guests.

Saigon

Ho Chi Minh City Vietnam

Kuala Lumpur Malaysia

Sydney Harbour Opera House Australia

29

The Cruises

ily and Billy weren't sure about dipping their toes into what they feared might be the potentially choppy waters of cruising. Billy had heard about a cruise that friends Raymond Divito and his wife Ann had been on in the Caribbean on a ship called the SS Norway, formerly the SS France. Billy says his initial reaction was that cruising would be a recipe for disaster in the shape of seasickness but Raymond assured him that the ship was so big 'it was like being on a floating island.' Lily agreed to give cruising a try and after flying to Miami the O'Neills boarded a ship nicknamed the Grand Dame the next day and enjoyed the cruise to the likes of Nassau in Bermuda, the US Virgin Island and St Thomas.

Queen Mary 2

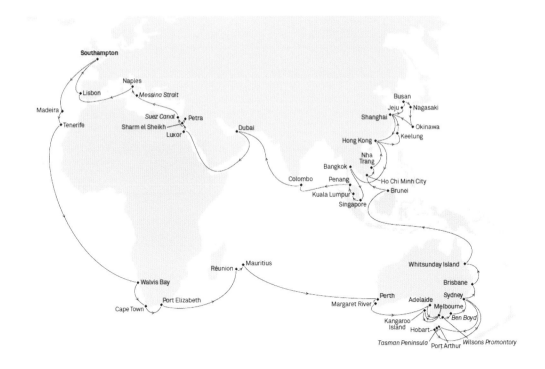

Queen Mary 2 World Voyage
10 January to 8 May 2017

"We enjoyed that first experience of cruising and resolved that we would be back," says Billy. Which they did big-time. They did return to the life on the ocean waves and their cruising itinerary read:

The Royal Caribbean Voyager of the Seas (with son Stephen and family). Oct 2003

NCL. Norwegian Jewel. November 2007

Carnival Freedom of the Seas. San Juan, Puerto Rico, St Thomas. Feb 2008

MSC Opera Italy. Craic on the Cruise. Sept 2008

Princess Cruises Island, Panama Canal. March 2009

Cunard QE2. Canary Islands (with friends Sam and Niki Moore). Nov 2009

Royal Caribbean. Oasis of the Seas (largest cruise ship afloat). Dec 2010

NCL . Norwegian Jewel of the Seas.

Rhine Cruise. October 2010.

Royal Caribbean. Adventure of the Seas, Western Mediterranean. July 2011

Carnival Miracle cruise. Fort Lauderdale. St Maarten, St Lucia, St Kitts. Feb 2012

NCL. Brilliance of the Seas. Baltic cities, St Petersburg Russia. June 2013

NCL. Norwegian Getaway. St Thomas, Tortola, Bahamas. April 2015

Celebrity Cruises. Celebrity Silhouette. Mexico, Jamaica, Haiti. Feb 2016

Holland America. Eurodam 4 cruise. Feb 2018

Caribbean Princess. Dec 2018-Jan 2019

Celebrity Silhouette. Dec 2019-Jan 2020

P&O Cruises. Iona. Spain and Portugal. (Celebrating Diamond Wedding Anniversary) Sept/Oct 2021

By the late 2000s Billy and Lily may have been old sea dogs having such a large number of cruises under their belts but nothing compared to the voyage that they embarked on in January 2017. For the world was about to literally become their oyster on a journey that took them right around the globe.

The cruise was to last an amazing 118 nights, stretching over 37,000 nautical miles, visiting 38 different ports in 22 countries on four continents. But the trip didn't start well as the O'Neills spent the night before departure on dry, very dry land, in a Southampton hotel that Billy says had more than a touch of the Fawlty Towers about it.

Billy and Lily had long waits for everything including for the fish and chips which was on the menu but arrived with no fish on the plate. On top of all that they were billed for the stay which they had actually pre-paid. However the next day was a different story as they boarded the Queen Mary 2, a spectacularly impressive luxury vessel that left the O'Neills awe-struck. After a welcome meeting in the Queen's Room with the captain, Kevin Oprey, Billy and Lily couldn't wait to explore the ship with the aid of a map that helped them navigate their way round the massive QM2 which had a choice of eight places to eat.

The O'Neills quickly found themselves at home. The food, the shows and the dancing – in the Queen's Room, the largest ballroom afloat - were all top drawer as was a casino and Billy and Lily loved dressing up in their finery for the formal dinners. Cunard even provided sharp-suited male dance partners for ladies who were on their own. Naturally enough, with Billy around, Lily didn't need to avail of their services.

The first three days of the cruise were spent at sea with the first port of call the exotic island of Madeira where Billy and Lily had spent a seven day holiday six months earlier. One of the must-dos in the capital Funchal for tourists was to have afternoon tea at the world famous Reid's Palace Hotel – a favourite holiday haven for former British Prime Minister Winston Churchill and Billy and Lily made a beeline for the clifftop treats.

The next stop on the cruise was another place that Billy and Lily knew well. They'd been to Tenerife no fewer than 15 times and even though Billy's wallet was stolen on one of their last visits the couple still went on a tour. After eight days at sea the QM2 arrived at Walvis Bay, Namibia where the attractions included the Namib desert and towering sand dunes and a museum.

Representatives of a large number of Rotary Clubs were also on the cruise and there were meetings and lunches for them and banners were exchanged by Billy on behalf of the Ballymoney organisation with other Rotarians.

At sea the O'Neills' days were spent sunbathing and swimming, reading books or playing darts while Billy attended talks on a wide range of subjects in a QM2 theatre. For smoker Lily there was only one dedicated area to have a puff – Billy dubbed it the 'coffin deck' The highlights of rest of the cruise read like a dream travelogue and some of them were meticulously recorded by Billy in a diary. And these are just some of them -

Jan 26 - Cape Town, South Africa. Shopping, bus tour, cable car trip up Table Mountain – terrific scenery.

Jan 29 - Port Elizabeth, South Africa. Five hour trip to a Game Reserve.

Feb 3 - Reunion Island. Island tour.

Feb 4 - Port Louise, Mauritius. Shopping all day. Vigil Mass on board at night.

Feb 12 - Freemantle, Australia. Train to Perth. Visit to State war memorial with three O'Neills remembered.

Feb 13 - Busselton. City famous for having the longest wooden pier in the Southern Hemisphere and a famous underwater observatory of sea life.

Feb 16 - Adelaide. Visit to Cleland wildlife park, home to koalas, kangaroos and wallabies.

Feb 18 - Melbourne. Hop on, hop off bus. Visit to massive Queen Victoria Market and the Crown casino.

Feb 20 - Kangaroo Island, Australia. Visit Seal Bay

Feb 22 - Melbourne again. Tram tour of city. Visit Eureka viewpoints.

Feb 23/24 - Wilson's Promontory/Ben Boyd national parks. Cruise by.

Feb 25 - Sydney. Train to suburb of Liverpool. Visit to Mary Laverty, the O'Neills' friend who worked for the Ford Hutchinson family at Stranocum Hall. Also had a lovely dinner with our son Terry's ex Ruth who now lives in Sydney.

Feb 27- Port Arthur. Guided tour of prison where deported convicts from England were once held. One of the deportees was a young boy who had stolen a handkerchief.

Feb 28 - Hobart, Tasmania, Shopping, walking and visit to a wildlife park.

March 2 - Sydney again. Visit famous Harbour Bridge and Sydney Opera House. Bus tour of city. Decide against going to Bondi beach 'because we see Burnside beach every day at home.'

March 4 - Brisbane. Visit family of Declan Rohdich son of our good friends Albert and Lily who went to school with Terry and Stephen. Driving tour of Gold Coast area.

March 5 - Airlie Beach. Relaxing day.

March 7 - Cairns (Yorkey's Knob terminal) . Cruise by Barrier Reef.

March 13 - Brunei. Visit Bandar Seri Begawan's wet and dry markets,

March 15 - Ho Chi Minh City, Vietnam. Sightseeing coach tour of city which has nearly nine million citizens and two and a half million scooters one of which Billy saw carrying a family of five while he heard some transported live bulls or cows on the back.

March 16 - Nah Tang, Vietnam. Visit market. Boat trip on the River Cai.

March 17 - At sea. St Patrick's Day gala party in the Queen's Room.

March 18 - Hong Kong. Billy has a strange experience as sees the lights of Hong Kong for the first time and wishes his mother and father could see them. At that moment a song came on the TV, I Dream of Jeannie with the Light Brown Hair which not only included his mother's name but was also one of her favourite songs. Toured Hong Kong on buses.

March 20 - Keelung, Taiwan. Walking tour of the National Palace Museum, and the colourful lantern streets.

March 22 - Shanghai, China. Visa needed to go ashore. Tour of the 'Best of Shanghai'. Walking tour of Jade Buddhist Temple, Shanghai museum, silk worm factory and the Yuyuan gardens. Boat trip on the Grand Canal which had people living on the water's edge in shacks. Human waste going into the canal.

March 24 - Busan (Pusan), South Korea Guided tour of Busan cultural centre where ladies were dressed in traditional costumes.

March 25 – Nagasaki, Japan. Visited the Atomic Bomb Museum and Hypocentre. No photographs allowed. Visit the Peace Memorial Park with its 30 feet high Statue of Peace. Emotional hymn singing and prayers. Tiring day ended with a snack in... an Irish pub of all places!

March 27 – Seoul. Visit to National Museum of Korea and guided tour of the Gyeongbokgung Palace.

March 29 - Shanghai again. Tour Garden City of Suzhou, Old Town and Nanjing Road shopping street.

April 1. Hong Kong again. Visit the 'Las Vegas of the East' Macau. Billy says his luck was out at the casinos.

April 5. Bangkok, Thailand. Bus tour; walking tour in grounds of Grand Palace but palace closed to foreign visitors because King of Thailand was lying in state for Thai citizens to pay their respects.

April 7/8 – Singapore. Visit to World Voyage dinner at the famous Mandarin Oriental Hotel followed by dancing. Afterwards Billy's knee seized up and medical staff advised him to have spa treatments and buy a walking stick. Day two visit to Changi prison chapel and Krangi war memorial. Hear stories of horrific treatment of prisoners who built the notorious Burma railway including Billy's uncle Hugh O'Neill who survived.

Ballroom on the Queen Mary 2

The O'Neills with Captain at formal reception

Winners of Masquerade Ball QM2

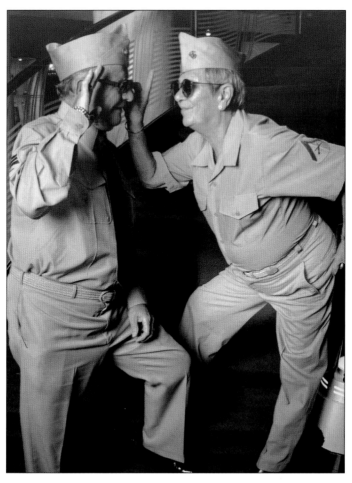

Winners of Fancy Dress board Queen Mary 2 World Cruise 2017

April 9 - Kuala Lumpur, Malaysia. Visit Suria KLCC shopping mall at the foot of Petronas Twin Towers. Over 300 shops in the six storey building.

April 10 - Penang, Malaysia Visit Georgetown, the Baba Nyonya Museum and Khoo Kongsi a Chinese Clan House.

April 13 - Colombo, Sri Lanka (formerly Ceylon) Visit to the Gangaramaya Temple, and Independence Square. Tuk tuk tour of a very busy city.

April 14/17 - At sea. Billy says grace at a Rotary lunch. Praises Rotary Clubs movement and borrowing an idea for another member Norman Rea says that he hopes his fellow members will never become 'Rice Krispie Rotarians' who are all snap crackle and pop before going limp but rather become 'full Irish breakfast Rotarians' that could sustain an army for a week.

April 18/19 - Dubai(United Arab Emirates) RAF helicopter escorted QM2 into port to deter pirates. Bus tour of city, visiting the Burj Al Arab Hotel and the Jumeirah Mosque, the Sheikh Zayed Road, the Manhattan of Dubai; the Museum, the Ambassador Lagoon Aquarium and the Gold Souk market. Followed by night tour.

April 20 - Muscat, Oman. Visit to shops. Reminded O'Neills of Tenerife.

April 21/24 - At sea. QM2 escorted at times by a British battleship to guard against pirates.

April 25 - Aqaba (for Petra), Jordan. Trip to Red City of Petra cancelled because of unrest in the area. Trip instead to a beach resort on the Red Sea. On return to QM2 security staff on main decks were armed with machine guns.

April 27 - Suez Canal/Port Said, Egypt.

April 28 - Limassol, Cyprus. Relaxing day at spa and shops.

May 1 - Messina Strait, Italy. Main shops closed because of holiday. Taxi to a tourist town 40 miles away. On return journey taxi has a puncture. Another cab gets passengers back to ship just in time for departure.

May 2 - Capri and Naples, Italy. Hair raising bus tour of Amalfi coast. Walking tour of Pompeii

May 3/4 - At sea. Final cocktail party. Billy and Lily win first prize in fancy dress competition in US Marine uniforms and dance the jitterbug to Bugle Boy Boogie.

May 5 - Lisbon, Portugal. Last port of call. Walk on promenade and shop in city for final souvenirs. Farewells at dinners and dances.

May 8- Southampton. Journey's end. Taxi to airport.

All in all Billy says he and Lily enjoyed their world cruise along with their 300 full-time guests and 2,000 additional travellers coming and going plus the 1200 staff. "But it was nice to be home safe and sound after such a lovely holiday with so memorable places having been visited," he adds.

30

On reflection. Looking back with Billy O'Neill

Billy O'Neill doesn't have to look too far if he wants to recall the memories and milestones in his colourful life. For as he sits in the office of his home in Portstewart all he has to do is to cast a glance around him to see photographs capturing the people and places that were important to him in his personal and professional life. Not that Billy needs too many aides memoire. For his recollection of details and places and dates is quite remarkable anyway. We're sitting in Billy's office re-visiting the highlights, and the lowlights, of his 80 plus years. And what better place to start than at the beginning in the Rodden Foot where Billy grew up.

Wedding of our granddaughter Arlene O'Neill to David Pudner and family Burton-on-Trent Cotswolds

I ask him if he harboured any boyhood ambitions back then about what he wanted to do with his life.

He says: "I had absolutely no idea of where I would end up or what I would become. I certainly had no notion that I would be where I am today. It's been nothing short of a miracle. Coming from a big family I always wanted to help out my mother especially after my father Ned passed away when I was just 15 months old. And I think that was why I was so keen to work even before I left school. I enjoyed helping with the family's ice-cream business where I was the go-for, seeking out the ice from Patterson's and the other ingredients from other shops. And when I wasn't doing that I sold newspapers or plucked chickens so that I could give my mother some money. Any other cash I had left for myself I spent on going to dances. I didn't smoke or drink and indeed I didn't have my first taste of alcohol until I was 28 years of age.

"Our home was a very happy one. There wasn't a lot of room to spare in the house. We were sleeping three to a bed or a bunk sometimes but I remember we were a big happy family. "Billy was a Catholic in a largely Protestant area. But he says that growing up in Ballymoney the religious tensions that had haunted Northern Ireland in its past and would do again in its future weren't a major concern in his youth. "No, religion really wasn't a problem for me," he says. "My mother came from a Protestant family and my grandfather was an Orangeman. My father was a Catholic but all my friends were Protestants and many of the friendships endured. Religion didn't enter anything apart from one night in the Top Hat/Strand Ballroom in Portstewart when the trumpet player Eddie Calvert started up Kevin Barry, a republican song that didn't go down well until he apologised, saying he thought he was in Ireland and no-one would take offence."

Billy says the early passing of his father meant that he wasn't able to be an influence in his life. But his mother Jeannie was a different story, altogether.

"She was a very big influence," he says. "She was a really busy woman but she had a heart of gold and she was very wise. The sage advice outlined at the start of this book, that my mother gave to me before I left Ballymoney to go over to work in England at the age of 16 was really important in shaping my outlook on life.

"Leaving Ballymoney and my family was a wrench, a tearful time but I enjoyed the idea of going to England even though I had no qualifications. I was determined to keep earning money to send home to my mother and I recall turning down the chance to go to a technical college because I would have lost a day's pay every week and that would have hit my mum in the pocket.

"I was lucky enough to have on-the-job training in the coming years working on the motorways in England and that stood me in good stead as I developed my career as a qualified fitter/mechanic. I enjoyed the work and I thought my life was destined to be spent in those kinds of roles and I never imagined the twists that would come along and take me back to Northern Ireland.

Billy worked in England at a time when stories were rife about people from Ireland experiencing difficulties and insults from local people. But he says he had no major issues, apart from making himself understood. He adds: "A lot of people couldn't make out what I was saying but I found it hard to understand what they were saying too, especially the Cockneys. I was encouraged to speak slower and more clearly. But I didn't experience any abuse because of where I came from, though it has to be said that on some of the contracts I was working on there were maybe 5,000 other Irishmen employed there too.

As Billy toiled on the motorways, wife Lily was primarily at home in a caravan looking after the O'Neills' two sons Terry and Stephen.

Billy says: "We couldn't have wished for a lovelier beginning to our marriage. We didn't have much but we had each other in the early days. I can still remember the first time I saw Lily in the Arcadia Ballroom. It really was love at first sight. Absolutely. I told Len Goodman exactly that on the TV show in 2019. And I quickly knew that I was going to marry her. We had some marvellous times, heading off for spins on my motorbike, going swimming and most of all going dancing, sometimes up to six nights a week. There was a lot of love between us and for Lily's mother Sally to tell me to stop seeing her was a real shock. I think she had realised that we were serious about each other and that marriage could be on the cards.

"We didn't decide there and then that we were going to elope. But the idea had been planted and one night I asked Lily how she felt about going away together. She said 'yes' and we decided on Glasgow because I knew a priest there and he gave me the address of a parochial house belonging to the Jesuits.

"When we went there we met Fr Langan for the first time. And he was an angel. He never judged us when we said we wanted to be married. He came from an Irish family and knew the pitfalls we could face as a couple from different religious backgrounds. Again we didn't ever envisage that we would establish a friendship with Fr Langan that would last right up until his death many, many years later and that he would come over to visit us in Ireland a number of times.

"Ironically Fr Langan was an engineer like me before he became a priest at the age of 21."

Billy describes his marriage to Lily as the best move he ever made. And his admiration for his wife still sparkles in his eyes as he talks about her, saying: "Lily has always been my backbone and in relation to the business side of things it didn't matter what I was buying like the first shop at Ballyreagh for £2,200 or the first caravan park at £40,000 she supported me completely.

"She had also backed the earlier decision to come home to Portrush from England after I broke my leg and I was laid up for six or seven months, living in a house that we had bought as an investment."

Once the O'Neills settled back permanently in Portrush, where the lure of the Arcadia Ballroom and high standard schools for the couple's sons were strong, relations with Lily's mother who had opposed their relationship in its infancy eased but Billy says she never apologised for her remarks though her husband Harry did 'with tears in his eyes.'

Even though Lily was a Protestant she took her sons to Mass when Billy was working as a mechanic.

Elaine and Gary O'Neill Wedding Day

Lily's mother Sally, brother Dennis and aunt Noel Gordon

Lily, her mum Sally with Conor, Terry and Stephanie

Stephen and Sandra O'Neill Wedding Castlerock

Sister Jean & Husband James Donnelly

"Many people thought Lily was a Catholic and that I was a Protestant," laughs Billy whose name, of course, re-enforced the public's erroneous perception about his religion.

Billy says living close to the Arcadia was a dream come true for the O'Neills and when they were able to recruit baby-sitters they made a beeline for the ballroom where they had lifetime passes.

He adds: "We loved the place and we were big fans of jiving in particular. My brother Hughie was a great jiver and brilliant at the jitterbug too. He learnt how to dance in a ballroom in Barry's Amusements where the ghost train was located in later years. I learnt how to jive from watching Hughie and my sister Jean. Not one step did I learn from a book or a class."

Billy and Lily perhaps could have danced at a higher level, at least on a more competitive basis but he says he was too busy building up his business to devote enough time to rehearsals.

But the couple did enjoy taking part in tournaments, especially on cruises. "On the four-month world cruise on the Queen Mary, Lily and I won four competitions between us. The ship has the biggest floating ballroom in the world and it was packed every night. We had taken some items with us and we won the top prize at a masquerade ball thanks to masks that we had bought in New Orleans. Lily won the Charleston contests which were women-only events and she was pictured with a huge bottle of champagne. Lily and I were also victorious at the fancy dress ball, wearing American GI uniforms. We were really proud to have won the competitions given that we were from such a small country like Northern Ireland while our rivals came from all around the world."

Back home as well as the Arcadia Billy and Lily have fond memories of other entertainment venues like the Cloonavin Hotel in Coleraine, the Old Mill in Bushmills, Strand Hotel Portstewart and Kelly's in Portrush where the couple were regularly asked to stage dancing demonstrations.

However when I ask Billy what one dance he would go back to if he had a time machine, he answers without hesitation, saying: "It would undoubtedly be the night that I met Lily in the Arcadia, dancing to Dave Glover. Dancing brought us together, we fell in love and we married and later renewed our wedding vows."

The irony in Billy's life is that after living in construction workers caravans in England in five years while he was working on the motorways, caravans would later become his livelihood and that his involvement with them would give him and his family a sound financially secure life.

"You couldn't have made it up," he says. "It all began when a guy from County Mayo whose machine I was repairing asked me if I knew anyone who would want to buy a caravan and I thought it would be a good starter home for my family after having enjoyed living with my brother and his wife. It was springtime in Kent where I was working. It was beautiful and being in that caravan was almost like a holiday for seven or so months before I traded it in for a bigger and better one. However I had no thoughts whatsoever that I would end up with a caravan business. And realistically I would probably have never built that business up if I hadn't lived in that first one. I might still have been a mechanic. But caravans did present a good life for me and Lily and my two sons and we ended up employing many people including members of our families."

Billy admits that his experience of caravan life in England taught him salutary lessons that would stand him in good stead in the future back home, adding: "One of the first things that I discovered was that if you didn't buy a caravan from the caravan park you usually didn't get onto it. But it also gave me an insight into the caravan industry and when I returned to Northern Ireland I was able to use that knowledge as I immersed myself more and more into the business side of caravans as I sold more and more caravans and bought caravan parks."

A clear source of lingering regret for Billy is that his plans to expand his Causeway Coast Hotel from 21 bedrooms to 101 bedrooms, beside the apartments he had built on the main road between Portrush and Portstewart, never came to fruition. And he's still frustrated that the tourism authorities wouldn't give him the support he says he needed, adding: "It was particularly galling because there was such a huge demand in the wider tourist market for the sort of bigger-scale hotel with a swimming pool and an exhibition centre that I was planning. I negotiated with the Tourist Board for seven or eight years; questions were asked in the House of Commons by the Rev Ian Paisley but at the end of the day it all came to nought.

Negotiating with the Tourist Board and Planning Service over all those years was extremely frustrating and it definitely has left a bad taste in my mouth especially as I was watching hoteliers coming in from outside Northern Ireland and getting virtually everything they asked for."

Billy went public with his concerns over his treatment but despite the headlines in newspapers it made no difference in what he called 'an unlevel playing field.' Billy says he had little alternative but to shelve the expansion plans and persisted with his smaller hotel until he sold it in 1998 after he received an offer he couldn't refuse.

Billy was thinking about using the proceeds to finance a deal to buy the Margoth caravan park in Portrush but he didn't get it, one of the few times that he failed in a move to add more parks to his portfolio.

"It was maybe a blessing in disguise that we didn't acquire the park. At the moment between all the family we now have about 700 caravan pitches in Northern Ireland. And better a fire that warms you than one that burns" Billy accepts that for someone who started life in a two-up-two-down house and later spent years living in caravans in England, a move to a Georgian mansion might sound like an unusual flit.

But as he reflects on his life Billy admits that one of his most fondly remembered achievements was the purchase and renovation of Stranocum Hall, not far from the village of Dervock.

To say the house had seen better days would be a massive understatement. The place had gone to rack and ruin only for John Stewart and his sons to renovate the shell, leaving the interior needing major work.

Kaelan, Conor, Terry, Stephanie, David, Sandra, Leanne, Stephen, Niall, Billy, Lily and Ryan

Niall, Kaelan, Arlene, Ryan, David and Conor

Stephen playing rugby

David O'Neill

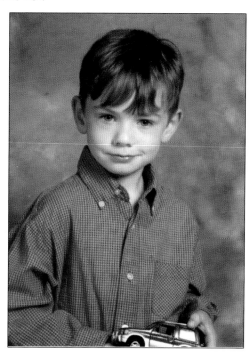

Conor O'Neill

I jokingly ask Billy if he looks back now and questions his own sanity he replies: "I suppose you could say that. But I do like a challenge and don't forget I had built the Causeway Coast Hotel from scratch. I had just sold the hotel when I bought Stranocum Hall from an estate agent called Uel Hammond. Working on Stranocum Hall was like a therapy to me. My sons might say that I went out there to graze but I had experience of building and design so I knew what I wanted for the inside of the House.

"As time went on at Stranocum it became apparent that the barn could be used as a centre for charities to stage fund-raising events. The Rotary Club held one and raised a lot of money and then the Lions Club wanted one and the Round Table wanted one. And then someone asked me if they could have a wedding at Stranocum too and I said yes on condition that the wedding party would give donations to charity.

"Down the years it was important for me to support good causes and to help people who were less fortunate than others."

Over the years Billy had persistent run-ins with the planning authorities over his proposals for a raft of developments, controversies that are detailed elsewhere in this book. During our conversations it's obvious that Billy is still hurt as he reflects on the sources of some of the opposition which was forwarded to the planners. He concedes: " I did perceive some animosity towards me in some of the property developments I was planning. I found out very quickly who my friends were. But I was particularly taken aback when I read the names of some of the people who objected to one of my proposals to build a housing development with 92 apartments and houses on Burnside Road in Portstewart."

Billy says he has always spoken his mind about what he considers to be the unfairness and lack of consistancy in the planning system in Northern Ireland and about his views on the way the tourism and hospitality sectors have been run in the past. And yes, he says, he did take some of the decisions that went against him personally.

But there's an obvious question. And that's why did Billy keep pushing ahead with his plans despite the regular roadblocks that appeared on his way? Was it stubbornness, pure and simple?

Billy says: "It was stubbornness and a bit of nerve really. When people said 'no' to me, my stubbornness kicked in and I resolved not to let them beat me, so I ploughed on and on."

Billy admits that the edict from Lily's mother, Sally that he couldn't marry her daughter because he was a Catholic and wouldn't prosper in Northern Ireland, also drove him on. "I was trying to prove a point that I could progress by being honest and hard-working, " says Billy who believes that he and his family have played a crucial role throughout Northern Ireland's troubles in giving people respite from the violence which raged for decades. When you think that we had 700 caravans with an average of two parents and two children in each of them, that's 2,800 people who were able to get away to the North Coast from the violence. You don't like to think that you gained from people's misfortunes when there was bombing in Belfast and Londonderry or wherever, but we were able to provide them with accommodation to get away from all that.

"I remember one bank manager who told me that he lived above his premises in Belfast and who said he often went to bed fully-clothed in the evenings in case the bank was bombed. But in the caravan on the North Coast he could find 'wonderful relaxation.' It was great to think that during those years of the troubles we were able to supply a lot of people with caravans where they could forget about their day to day worries. And many, many professional people were customers of ours. One surgeon who bought a number of caravans from us down the years loved the lifestyle away from the pressures in his hospital so much that he decided to buy a house and re-settle permanently on the North Coast. He was later to tell me his only problem in having a full-time home up here meant that he had nowhere to go on his weekends! "

Wearing his old Causeway Coast Hotel hat, Billy says that he used to be annoyed that hotels in Northern Ireland were obliged to stay open all year round when the winter season made it unprofitable to keep their doors open.

He adds: "I put to the Tourist Board that our hotels should do what some of their counterparts in the south did – and that was to close maybe for a few months of the year. I was told that the difficulty lay with the fact that our hotels might lose their 12 month licences. But that didn't make a lot of sense to me. "

Even today, decades after Billy's proposals for an expanded Causeway Coast Hotel fell through, he still has concerns about 'the lack of vision' in the way the tourist industry is being run on the north coast especially in the hotel sector. Many newspaper column inches have been filled in recent years with stories about plans for new and more substantial hotels to be constructed to meet the constant demand for bedrooms, plans which have been subjected to legal challenges in the courts. Says Billy: "They're still crying out for a 100 bedroom hotel in Portrush that could take coach parties and the like. Frustrating wouldn't be the word for it, really."

Given the number of problems that Billy had with officialdom down the years and his tough talking, I ask him if he ever considered becoming a politician to use his experiences to help other people.

The answer comes quickly. "Not once," he says. "A good businessman from Ballymena who was a friend of my father's told me a long time ago that I should never go into politics. He said it would be better to get to know politicians and let them do all the shouting for me! I think that's one of the best pieces of advice I ever got but I never took it."

I ask Billy if there was a secret to his success in the caravan business. He says: "Other park owners used to ask me how I managed to acquire such a good clientele onto my parks and I always said it was because I treated people right. And because I was a mechanic in the past I was able to maintain high standard myself and introduce improvements, putting in water, sewerage and electricity for my customers on my own. "

So much for Billy's successes, I then ask him what his biggest regrets in his private or commercial life are. And again the response comes swiftly. "I am sorry that I never knew my father who died when I was so young. I don't have any recollections of him at all or of my grandparents who lived in Ballymena. But I had a really happy life in Ballymoney. In the

Family album

Family album

Rodden Foot no-one ever locked their doors. You were able to go into people's houses and have a chat. It was wartime, of course, but everyone was very friendly in our area. I would have gone up the street for the messages from Getty's shop and I remember seeing people happily dancing at the crossroads with Church Street. That's how relaxed life was. There was a great spirit and people seemed to move on with life even though there was a war going on. I wasn't a big football watcher but I did enjoy taking part in kick-abouts on the Green near my home and we would also have played cricket too with the most basic of equipment.

"After the war was over I didn't have a lot of time to myself in my childhood because when our family ice cream business was thriving I was busy with it before I got a few other jobs to help out my mother."

I ask Billy what he hopes his legacy will be. And again he responds without hesitation: "My motto has always been 'family first.' My legacy going out of this world would be the knowledge that I have left my family have nothing to worry about."

His family are all important to Billy and it's obvious that they reciprocate the feelings. Among Billy's many volumes of treasured letters and papers a laminated note he received on his 79th birthday from grandson Conor stands out.

Conor wrote: "I want to tell you how much I love you and thank you for all you do for me. Not many kids had a childhood like mine from going to auctions, to building Con Air (models) out of timber in your garage and the endless number of other memories I have. Your love and support never fade. You and Nanny's influence in my life has been monumental. I can never thank you enough. All I can say is that I love you from the bottom of my heart and I'm proud to call you my granddad."

I ask Billy if he is a Christian and he replies: "Absolutely. My faith is important to me. I may not go to church every day as a lot of people do. As regards Lily if anyone asks her what religion she is, she simply says that she's a Christian.

"I remember that a solicitor once told me that when I was trying to obtain planning for this, that and the other that my problem was that I was too honest. If I see a man who has a massive million pound yacht and if he has worked hard for that I say 'good luck to him, he deserves it.'

"But if a gangster like the Russian President Vladimir Putin who has palaces, cars and planes with a salary that is supposed to be a hundred thousand a year then I will ask how he got that money, that property and the planes. I have had great satisfaction in giving away a lot of money to support charities and sporting events like the Milk Cup and the North West 200 as well as organisations like the NSPCC which is my favourite good cause.

"As well as assisting charities I have also been proud to be part of organisations like the Round Table, the Rotary Club and the Lions Club. I was able to give them my time and help them come to the aid of great charities."

Nowadays Billy has few personal financial worries. But he laughs: "I have assets which are obviously worth a considerable amount of money but I'm certainly no billionaire."

He adds: "Many people have a lot of assets which have come from money that has been lent to them. But I have no bank borrowing. I enjoy the fruits of my labour. I like driving around in my car (a Bentley) and my wife and I enjoy cruising because it means that Lily doesn't have to cook so much. We still like going out with friends and family at home too. And I would just as soon enjoy a holiday in a caravan as I would in a five star hotel. "

Good friends Cecil Graham LVO OBE and his wife June

Billy's mother with her two sisters and his brother James and sister-in-law Joan

Jake Adair age two our step great gandson

31

Praise from a veteran journalist

Coleraine journalist W. Speedy Moore was one of Northern Ireland's best-known and best-loved writers. He was for 68 years a much-read columnist on the Coleraine Chronicle. And he could turn his hand to any subject, big or small. Among his most eagerly-read articles were ones which took a nostalgic look back at the past. He was also a self-avowed fan from childhood of the ice-cream made by Billy O'Neill's family. And Speedy dedicated a large section of one of his books to their wares. He wrote: "We looked forward to one special luxury from April to September - Ned O'Neill's ice cream which was sold in the form of ha'penny and penny sliders.

Speedy Moore

For the respectable sum of tuppence an enormous portion was served, with the hearty vendor calling it a 'bumper' and wishing the buyer good luck. As we only had pocket money on Saturday mornings Ned fitted his visits to suit that sparse economic situation and we awaited his arrival with watering teeth. Ned was born in Ballymena and though no court trumpets heralded his arrival Royal blood flowed through his veins. His clan can be traced back to Eoghan, son of the 5th century Niall of the Nine Hostages, a sept which is one of the oldest surnames in Ireland. O'Neill has been in continuous use since King Domhnall in the 10th century.

The story goes that Edward O'Neill befriended an old Italian and helped him stabilise his business against strong opposition. When the Italian died he bequeathed to the good Samaritan an ice cream recipe said to have been a secret in the old man's family for generations. Edward started making and selling ice cream in Ballymena but after a while decided to move to Ballymoney a town he had a liking for. He and his wife Jeannie settled in well with the people of the Route who had a craze for taking shortcuts. They cut the newcomer's name from Edward to Ned and forever more it remained plain Ned."

Speedy went on to relate how Ned had 'only the security of his meagre savings and initiative to help him in an uncertain future.' He also said he wasn't afraid of hard work starting his operations at 4am seven mornings a week.

Speedy wrote of how Ned's sons helped their father and how the business prospered with the purchase of a piebald pony and cart, one of many he bought to build up a fleet 'with the carts magnificently decorated in bright paints' helping his ice cream to become a household name in a large part of Northern Ireland.

The book also covered Billy's brother Leo winning 'against all odds' the Ulster light-heavyweight boxing championship in 1945 and how Ballymoney celebrated by lighting bonfires in his honour.

Speedy wrote of the mourning at Leo's passing in 1994 and how people shared memories of a youthful Leo selling ice-cream from a 'fully loaded box bicycle' in Ballymoney, Coleraine, Portrush and Portstewart before 'with the call of the rooster the next morning he would ride his machine to Ballycastle and no living soul ever heard him utter one word of complaint. He was truly of the O'Neill breed.'

After his death, Speedy, who described Leo as a long-time friend, penned a heartfelt personal obituary to him in his newspaper column saying: "Leo has crossed the vale of shadows and it is sad that we will no longer have the pleasure of his breezy company. But those folk who knew him will always have nice memories of him – rest peacefully good friend. In his book Speedy Moore also paid tribute to Billy O'Neill, writing "Remarkable business success was achieved by a younger member of the O'Neill family. I refer to Billy. One memorable summer he obliged a friend by letting the family caravan to him. Year after year the plan developed and the result was a spacious fully-equipped caravan park at Portstewart, a unique holiday apartment service and the imposing Causeway Coast Hotel, overlooking the Atlantic on the Portrush-Portstewart Road. The spirit of progress at its best."

Tributes from Billy and Lily's sons
Stephen and Terry O'Neill

I'm delighted that Dad has risen to the challenge of collaborating with Ivan Little on writing a book on the Billy and Lily O'Neill story. I'm expecting it to be along the lines of the old TV series "This Is Your Life" that we used to watch and enjoy as a family back in the 70s sitting in front of a black and white TV with 3 channels- only no Eamonn Andrews holding a big red book this time.

Having just turned 60 myself it's going to be impossible (but I will try) to briefly convey what a massive positive influence my parents have been throughout the years and continue to be to our expanding family which has mushroomed now to include grandkids and great grandkids. Literally, I along with my 3 boys Conor, Kaelan & Niall wouldn't be here without my parents and come to think of it my wife Stevie (Stephanie) would be off the hook!

I remember vividly our early days living in a small caravan (which seemed so big to me) on a construction site as Dad was working on building the motorways in England. At the time living in the middle of a construction site was a great adventure/education for a young kid. By the time I was five I knew the names of all the plant and equipment Dad was working on and thought nothing of seeing Mum plucking a Pheasant that Dad had hunted in the nearby woods. I have since learned that mum hated plucking pheasants (lol.)

These early childhood memories must have rubbed off as to this day my hobby is pulling apart old cars and rebuilding them and not plucking pheasants!! However I do miss the pheasant feathers as they were great for making Indian headdresses.

When I was five and starting school, we moved into our first house in Causeway Street, Portrush and I couldn't believe how massive it was. I remember running up the stairs and shouting down to my brother Stephen to come up quick because "there are beds up here".

Mum and Dad showed as much love as any parents could and loved telling Stephen and me bedtime stories about a fictional Kogi Bear with stories they made up. But boys being boys, just occasionally, I might have been a bit mischievous and my parents' discipline was swift and fair and thankfully they didn't catch me too often!

Together Mum and Dad are quite a force. Nothing ever came easy but they managed 60 years of marriage and built a successful business from the ground up which is testimony to their resolve. I couldn't be prouder of them

After selling the hotel side of the business I thought they would take things a bit easier. I was right to some degree as after a lifetime of working 60–70-hour weeks their newfound freedom gave them a chance to pursue the activities they enjoy. One of those activities was giving back to the community by way of charity fundraising and on numerous occasions they opened their home hosting many events including barbecues. It was great when their efforts were recognised as the Queen awarded Dad an MBE.

Over the years it became obvious Mum and Dad have a great sense of fair play and love to give advice. So much so that they have mastered it to the point where they can administer it in one sentence.

So here are a few of the many nuggets of wisdom they came out with over the years that have stuck with me.

*Remember the people you meet on the way up are the same people you

meet on the way down.

*It's nice to be important but it's more important to be nice.

*You'll never plough a field turning it over in your mind.

*Good manners cost nothing.

*You're not as green as you're cabbage looking.

(Actually it was my uncle Eddie O'Neill that I worked with on the caravan parks that started saying that and it always made me laugh).

Mum and Dad, along with my much-loved grandparents Harry and Sally encouraged me a great deal and instilled a sense of how to get on with things and keep going. And that has come in handy over the last 60 years.

With only 20 years between the generations, I used to get annoyed when in my late teens people would think Mum was my sister and Dad my brother. This was especially true as I worked as a teen in the Strand Hotel, Portstewart as a barman/night porter when Mum and Dad would be in the function room dancing the night away to Plug and Dom.

Anyway, I'm over it now and long may they continue to get younger as I get older!! My love and respect go out to Mum and Dad and a big thank you to them for all they have done and continue to do.

Terry O'Neill and his wife Stephanie wedding 8th-March-1996

Terry O'Neill

My earliest memory of my Dad is from when I was about three or four years old. It was in our house in Causeway Street in Portrush. Mum had taken me into the bedroom to see Dad who had returned from working in England after he had broken his leg. I remember the bedsheets were held up to keep the pressure off his legs.

I later learned that Dad had almost died from a clot from his accident but thankfully he pulled through and beat the odds that were stacked against him. I realise now how lucky we were because as a child Dad had lost his father who was working in England.

I often think about Dad's rise from being a mechanic to a successful businessman and now MBE and it's something that I would often quote when my own customers inquire about how I got into the caravan trade. I explain to them how my father created his business from working as a mechanic and having a tuck shop out of a suitcase at work to then spotting an opportunity to having a shop on a caravan park.

He then converted a caravan with his own hands, and I think of the enjoyment I had working alongside him from building our bunk beds, wardrobes and even fitting out shops and serving in them as an eight or nine year old.

I thought there wasn't anything my dad couldn't do. For most children when they grow up they discover that's not the case. But not for me.

From selling caravans Dad excelled and moved onto buying caravan parks and building the most modern parks 45 years ago, having chalet lodges with double glazing and central heating and pipe gas when other caravans were still using gas lights and outside WCs.

After this Dad moved his sights, building the first purpose-built award-winning apartments, followed by a hotel - as I say there's not a lot he couldn't do.

Dad's qualities far exceeded his business and entrepreneurial skills. As a teenager growing up Dad was a jacket, shirt and tie man. Always tidy and meticulous, I've never heard an obscene comment or a foul word from his mouth.

Mum and Dad are well known for their talents on the dance floor, it wasn't uncommon to be out at a disco and the DJ would announce "clear the floor for Billy and Lily O'Neill".

While I would like to think I acquired some of my dad's qualities, dancing was not one of them.

I remember being told a story about a German man who had recognised Mum and Dad on a holiday 20 years after seeing them dancing in Majorca. That's the sort of presence and charisma they have.

Dad has always worked hard and played hard and was fair across the board.

He befriended everyone he met – from the priest who married them to the American hitchhiker he met on the way to the Giant's Causeway.

Dad still surprises me in what he can accomplish. At the age of 70 he set up a home in America and passed his driving test in Florida and now he's told Ivan Little his story for a new book about his and Mum's lives together.

I feel I have been privileged in having a role model and a father such as mine. And I am thankful for the opportunities passed onto me.

Stephen O'Neill

Grandson Ryan enjoying a holiday at Disneyworld with Mum, Dad Granny and Granda

32

In poetic praise of the old Rodden Foot

I t mightn't be quite up to standard of Seamus Heaney, John Keats or William Wordsworth but a poem about Billy O'Neill's old street in Ballymoney still strikes a chord with people who used to live in the Rodden Foot. The writer calls it the Rodden Foot but while he spells it as one word rather than the two normally associated with the street there's no mistaking his affection for it. Billy, however, has no idea about the identity of the poet. "A farmer near Stranocum Hall lent me a book and the poem was in it, " he says. Old characters from the Rodden Foot like the blacksmith Hughie Wade and the tinsmith Alex Mills are brought to life in the twelve verses of the poem. And the O'Neills' ice cream also gets a mention as do shops belonging to Miss Beverland and James Getty.

Rodden Foot

THE OLD RODDEN FOOT

In a scheme of redevelopment
There has vanished from the Route
The old-time row of houses
Known as the Rodden Foot.
A landmark of our native town
Of toil and civil trade
Where all of our forefathers
An honest living made.

It really seems like yesterday
Since I walked around the street
With lots of my companions
All marching with bare feet
For money it was hard to find
And decent jobs were few
But with care and simple living
We managed to get through.

It is with very solemn thoughts
Those days I now recall
For many of those school pals
Cannot be found at all.
Some wonder in a foreign land
With fame and fortune blessed
They have said goodbye Rodden Foot
Where once they were oppressed.

In dreams I see Miss Beverland's shop
Right close up to Queen Street
And of't when we were feeling blue
To it we did retreat
Sometimes the lady pitied us
And give us each a gum
We thought it just the greatest thing
Until the kingdom come.

Hughie Wade he was the blacksmith
How he made the anvil ring
And as he shod the horses
We could often hear him sing
If music pleased the customer
Even though the corn was ripe
Hughie often took a minute
Just to play the old bagpipes

I picture now James Getty's shop
To us the centre store
I see him as if yesterday
Looking o'er the wee half door
His friendly smile and cheerie word
To neighbours was a treat
But the highlight I remember
Was the penny worth of sweets

The Rodden Foot could always boast
Of many arts and skills
We had a Tinsmith of our own
T'was brave wee Alex Mills
He made our cans and kettles
The pin tins by the score
Including all the oddities
We used in days of yore

Some neighbours used to keep a pig
The better off kept two
The thrifty folk twelve laying hens
The sportsman kept a Grue
And when needed to spring clean
To keep the back yard smart
We had our own disposal works
In Tweed's old Clabber cart

Now in a busy season
When the farmer sowed his seed
Quite often there was work for all
To help and plant or weed
And when the spuds were being dug
There was lots of work to do
Around Kirkhills and Druckendult
And out around Culdoo

But now the Rodden Foot has gone
I wish that I could find
The neighbours of those bygone days
Who these stories bear in mind.
We must have been a healthy crowd
That hard times did not kill
As the very best of folk we tried
In McClearys Spinning Mill

So we'll say goodbye to the Rodden Foot
The fowl men and their art
To little ice cream Johnnie
Likewise his ice cream cart.
We'll hear no more the gamecocks crow
Around the cockpit brae
Or go in search of ponies
That have wandered far away.

The poorhouse Burn no more we'll see
It's all packed up quite neat
A lovely library feels the spot
Where once the goats did bleat
The Old Folks Home looks very nice
T'was planned by brains from Route
But to me could never take the place
Of the Old Rodden Foot.

(Source unknown)

226

Lays of Ancient Ballymoney

What means this wild confusion, this sound of marching feet
Why all this wild commotion resounding down the street
What can it mean but trouble, in Stuart's fair domain
The Clansmen of the Rodden Foot are in the wars again!

As usual McCotter is foremost in the field
A Chieftain skilled in Civic strife, and never known to yield
He, and his angry legions, will be very hard to stop
As he leads these yelling warriors to William Stuart's shop.

And lo, within the kitchen, sits the Chieftain of Clan Boyle
A hawk who loves the battle – but only for the spoil
He hears the din approaching, but does not leave his seat,
He mans the post of danger – because he can't retreat!

And Johnny Brown, who sits with him, feels stirring in his heart
A sudden wish, to see again, his home in fair Drumart
He gird his loins, and hied him off, too well he knew that sound
And did not wish to interfere – with Magistrates around!

But Stuart's eyes are anxious now, when will this warfare stop
A crash and now McCotter is standing in the shop.
"Here Stuart take this message to R D's Sunday class" he said
And seizing Stuart's scales, he hurled them through the glass!

In days of knightly glory – in Coeur de Lion's day,
What Knight threw down his gauntlet, in such a warlike way
Against the blindfold Goddess, the bold McCotter rails
There was a note symbolic, in throwing down the scales!

What boots it now that Stuart in fleeing in defeat
That Boyle's smooth and oily tongue is covering his retreat
On Monday, outraged, justice, the flames if war will quench
And a very meek McCotter will cringe before the bench?

P Boyle

33

Billy and Lily O'Neill... A timeline

May 19, 1960. Billy and Lily meet in the Arcadia Ballroom, Portrush.

June, 1961. Move to live and work in Glasgow.

September 23, 1961. Married by Fr James F. Langan SJ in St Aloysius Church, Glasgow

November 1961. Go to live with Billy's brother Hugh in Kent.

March 4 1962. Son Terry born

May, 1962. Buy first home, a £45 caravan.

August 25 1963. Son Stephen born.

A visit to Graceland

1967 . Move back to Northern Ireland. Billy works on M2 Ballymena by-pass Buy house in Causeway Street, Portrush. Start in hospitality industry by sub -letting caravan at Skerry View caravan park.

Feb 15 1971. Buy Ballyreagh Stores, Portrush

March 1974. Buy Burnside Caravan Park, Portstewart

1976. Buy Castlerock Holiday Park.

March 1976. Buy one and a half acre site at Cashlandoo, Portstewart for caravan sales.

1977. Buy farm at Mill Road, Portstewart and build Portstewart Holiday Park.

1977. Buy house and two acres of land for development at 36 Ballyreagh Rd, Portstewart

1984 Sell two caravan parks to son Terry and Stephen .

1985. Build Causeway Coast Apartments for rentals.

1986. Build O'Neill's restaurant, Ballyreagh.

1991. Build Causeway Coast Hotel, Ballyreagh.

Jan 1998. Sell Causeway Coast Hotel and Apartments.

1998 Buy Stranocum Hall. Refurbish house and Bell Tower barn and outhouses into a small museum

Sept 2001. Renew wedding vows on 40th anniversary with Fr Langan performing the ceremony in St John the Baptist Church, Dervock where Billy's mother and father were married

October 25 2005. Buy Edgewater Holiday Park, Minerstown, County Down with nephew Loren and his wife Lin.

March 2017. Move from Stranocum Hall to Ocean Green, Portstewart.

October 25, 2017. Sold share of Edgewater Holiday Park to Loren and Lin.

February 26, 2020. Go off alcohol for lent. Still off it.

September 25, 2021. Nephew Gary O'Neill sadly passes away.

October 28, 2021. Death of musician Gay McIntyre who had been a favourite of the O'Neills and played at Billy's 70th birthday in the Royal Court Hotel Portrush.

November 28, 2021. Billy's 82nd birthday, Water Margin, Coleraine.

January 3, 2022. Caribbean cruise for five weeks.

February 11, 2022. Lily's 80th birthday. Surprise party for 33 family and friends.

February 22, 2022. Visit Lily's mother Sally's grave in Armagh on what would have been her 100th birthday. Leave a stone painted by Terry's wife Stephanie, saying 100 kisses on your birthday. 'The original when Harry met Sally.'

March 10, 2022. Billy has skin lesions removed at Causeway Coast Hospital.

34

Top of the Pops and All that Jazz

Billy O'Neill's love of his family and his enthusiastic pursuit of success in business haven't been the only passions in his life. Jiving and jazz have also been music to his ears. And Billy remembers many of the dances and concerts he and Lily attended with astonishing clarity. Indeed he's drawn up a top 30 (plus) of his favourite gigs and the tunes that struck a chord with him. So, as they say in all the best TV shows in no particular order, here goes – starting with the venue followed by the name of the musician(s) and the stand-out song or instrumental.

The Royal Showband

Ballymoney Orange Hall... Hugh Tourish (In The Mood)

Ballymoney Town Hall... Clipper Carlton Showband (When The Saints Go Marching In)

Ballymena Town Hall... Johnny Quigley All Stars (South Rampart Street Parade)

Coleraine Town Hall... Royal Showband (Tiger Rag)

Newry Town Hall... Dave Glover Showband (Skin Deep)

Dundalk Town Hall... Capitol Showband (Ice Cream)

Armagh City Hall... The Cadets Showband (Marching Through Georgia)

Warrenpoint Town Hall... Chris Barber Jazz Band (Royal Garden Blues)

Chatham Town Hall... Acker Bilk Jazz Band (Woodchoppers' Ball)

Londonderry Guildhall... Kenny Ball Jazz Band (High Society)

Boathouse Coleraine... Ken Colyer Jazz Band (Didn't He Ramble)

Cloonavin Coleraine... Alex Welsh Jazz Band (Jazz Band Ball)

Palais de Dance, Portstewart... Graham Stewart Jazz Band (Jitterbug Boogie)

Top Hat Ballroom, Portstewart... Paddy Cole Jazz Band (Chimes Blues)

Strand Ballroom, Portstewart... Eric Delaney Big Band (Equinox)

Arcadia Ballroom, Portrush... Joe Loss Jazz Band (Hiawatha Rag)

Palladium Ballroom, Portrush... Ted Heath Jazz Band (Little Brown Jug)

Flamingo Ballroom, Ballymena... John Anderson Jazz Band (Wonderful World)

Muff Ballroom, Co. Donegal... Clyde Valley Stompers (Don't Fence Me In)

Pageant Ballroom, Kent... Jimmy Compton All Stars (Guitar Boogie Shuffle)

Casino Ballroom, Kent...Wood Choppers Showband (Jump and Jive)

Co-op, Rochester, Kent... Monty Sunshine (Cherry Pink)

Ronnie Scott's London... Trevor Keys Duo 2T's (Lady In Red)

Hammersmith Palais... Apex Jazz Band (Dance The Night Away)

Lyceum Ballroom... Billy White Jazz Band (Twist tunes)

Royal Albert Hall... George Melly (Cha Cha)

Cotton Club, Glasgow... Stephane Grappelli (Latin American tunes)

Roseland Ballroom, New York... The Music of Glenn Miller (GI Bugle Boy)

Cork Jazz Festival... Barrel House Jazz band (Barrelhouse Showboat)

O'Neill Suite. Plug and Dominic (Equinox)

Derry Jazz Festival...The Jive Five (I Am Yours)

PS. Cruise Ships... Dancing To The Music of Louis Armstrong; Count Basie, Duke Ellington and Jelly Roll Morton.

35

The war time reflections

The producers of an archive called Our Lives to mark the 60th anniversary of the end of the Second World War in 2009 turned to Billy O'Neill as one of the people to help them record their memories from Derry, the North-West and the Causeway regions of Northern Ireland. The idea was to put together a collection of personal stories from the area from the late 1930s to 1950s and an exhibition was also designed to open in tandem with a publication setting out ' everyday things like fashion, the roles of women and children, housing transport, emigration, agriculture and the social revolution in youth culture and entertainment.'

Barrow in Furness blitz 1941

Festival of Britain Party

The publication, organisers said, was to provide a wide range of material – oral history excerpts, photographs and documents - for schools and community groups exploring the legacy of WW2.

Billy was a natural choice. He had been born in November 1939 not long after the outbreak of war and though he clearly didn't have too many stories to tell about the start of hostilities he was more than able to share memories of growing up in the latter years and after the war was over.

Billy's submissions to the publication ranged from happy days to sadder ones. Uppermost in his reflections was the death of his father Ned during the war in England in 1941 when Billy was 15 months old.

Billy recalled: "He was over in Barrow on Furness putting roofs back onto factories that the Germans had bombed, factories that were building submarines. He caught pleurisy. He was only 46. My oldest brother Leo was working in England at the time. He got a telegram telling him to attend the funeral in England."

Billy reflected on how his mother's twin brother James also died from pleurisy at the age of 26.

People who were surveyed for the project were asked to reflect on the people who mattered to them from WW2 and leaving aside his family Billy replied: "I think about the people who died during the war so that we could live." Asked about his abiding memories from the post-war years Billy said:"My mother got free national dried milk and they collected it from a clinic in Queen Street, Ballymoney. You got orange juice too for vitamins and of course, we got free milk at school."

Billy also spoke about helping out during his earliest schooldays with the O'Neill family ice cream manufacturing business and about how at one time there were five horse and carts selling their products. He also recalled how his mother Jeannie was the driving force behind the entire operation and how the smallest ice cream on offer was a threepence slider and the largest a sixpenny one.

Turning to how people had enjoyed themselves as children Billy said occasional outings to places like Portrush and Downhill as seven and eight-year-olds were the highlights of the year, sometimes making the journey on the family's horse and traps.

Billy lamented the fact that he had had to leave school at the age of 14 to help provide for his family. He told Our Lives that he missed not having had more education.

He talked about how he took a number of jobs near his home and later worked at Balnamore Mill near Ballymoney as a 'cage boy' for £3 a week before being made redundant and going to work in Britain.

Billy told the archivists that unemployment was rife and most of his brothers headed across the water to find work.

It probably wouldn't have been Billy O'Neill if his reminisces didn't focus on his dancing. And he told   Our Lives how he used to enjoy getting the acclaim from other dancers as they applauded the efforts of him and his partners in ballrooms like the Arcadia in Portrush. Billy also said that the jiving and jitterbug skills of many of the local dancers were learnt from the visiting American servicemen who brought their love of big band music with them to Ireland.

Billy said that there was no alcohol on sale in the dance halls. "People just didn't drink. They danced all night," he added. Eight years later Billy and Lily were featured in a BBC Radio Ulster series in which older people spoke about their experiences. It was called The Time of Our Lives.

But Lily started off the conversation by saying that the first time she met Billy in the Arcadia Ballroom in 1960 wasn't all champagne and roses.

Thinking back to her first encounter with the man who would become her husband she said: "He asked me for a dance so I got up and he said 'you'll do alright, I'll teach you. You're like a big plough horse at the moment."

Interviewer Colm Arbuckle said: "There must have been something you fancied." And Lily replied: "Well, it wasn't his suit. He had on a pink suit and I didn't realise it was pink. I thought it was a natural colour and it wasn't until about three weeks later when he showed me a button that had come off the suit which cost him a fortune that I saw it was pink."

Billy then told Colm that the Arcadia years were a golden era for dancing and for bands, adding: "Absolutely wonderful. We used to come in at nine o'clock at night and we wouldn't have missed a dance until half one or possibly two in the morning. But my first time in the Arcadia I was about 15 – it

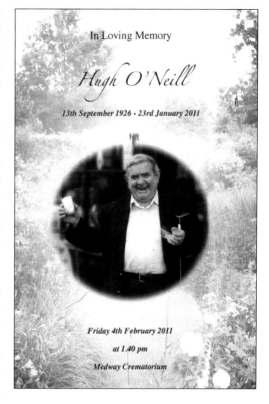

In Loving Memory

Hugh O'Neill

13th September 1926 - 23rd January 2011

Friday 4th February 2011

at 1.40 pm

Medway Crematorium

was before I met my wife in 1960. It was a Christmas Eve and unfortunately I missed the bus back to Ballymoney. And I had to walk all the way, 12 or 13 miles, back to Ballymoney."

Billy said all his brothers and sisters enjoyed dancing and he added: "It was about the only thing you had to do around Ballymoney, Portrush, Portstewart and Coleraine in those days."

The Epilogue

The words that Billy O'Neill's mother and his mother-in-law said to him in his youth echoed in his ears throughout his life. They were good and bad. Jeannie O'Neill had told her 16 year old son that good manners and honesty should be his bywords in life. But in the early days of his relationship with Lily, her mother Sally warned him bluntly to stay away from her daughter telling him that as a Catholic he would never succeed in Northern Ireland. But he says: "Within 28 years I was employing Lily's mother, her father, her brother and his wife and their two children. And I was also employing upwards of 14 of my own family. Plus by 1990 I was employing more than 100 people and building a hotel from scratch. So I reckoned I got on alright.

STRICTLY FOR Billy + Lily
Yours A "TEN" FROM LEN !

"And what I want to say is my philosophy is that if you are willing to work and have a bit of a nerve you can get on in Northern Ireland or anywhere else," says Billy who's admitted that he's learnt a lot of hard lessons about life and business through his remarkable career. And he concedes that he may sometimes have been too trusting, something that was underlined by the case of a former friend and financier who defrauded him of over £100,000 in an investment scam.

Although this traumatic episode was a major disappointment, Billy prefers not to dwell on the setbacks and instead counts his blessings for what has come his way particularly with his beloved family. Billy also says that his and Lily's story is an example of what two ordinary people, from different religious backgrounds in Northern Ireland, can achieve, even against the tide.

He adds: "I said at our 60th wedding anniversary celebration that the moral of our story was that no matter what religion you are if you are honest and prepared to work hard – and you also have friends and family behind you like we had – you can get on in Northern Ireland. I also said that I hoped that Sally was listening 'up there'

DESIGN • PRINT • PUBLISHING • DISTRIBUTION

CEDRIC WILSON

Designed & Published by Cedric Wilson
Email: cedricwilson@live.co.uk